16 Modern Studies for Flamenco Guitar

Yago Santos

To access the video go to:
WWW.MELBAY.COM/31033V - YOUTUBE
DV.MELBAY.COM/31033 - DOWNLOAD

To access the audio go to:
WWW.MELBAY.COM/31033MEB

WWW.MELBAY.COM

TABLE OF CONTENTS

To my family and friends

Preface

The study of flamenco guitar technique can be a bit tedious if you do not have the appropriate exercises and study routine. Studying with a noteworthy teacher can be of great help to the student, but if you do not have such a guide or opportunity—as with any musical instrument—organization and discipline are essential for progress.

Personally, I like to approach the study of the guitar according to my current level of development; having played at a good level for 15 or 20 years, I no longer play the same exercises I did as a beginner. In the beginning stages, I recommend the ongoing study of foundational exercises to strengthen the "muscles" of both hands, not only to achieve greater speed and ease of play, but also to work on tone, time and other fundamentals of musicianship. This first stage can be compared to an athlete who needs to perform certain exercises in the gym for hours each day, just to strengthen his or her body and empower it for a specific activity.

Once you have played for a few years, you should identify your strengths and weaknesses as a guitarist to focus your energies on the latter. At this stage, it is very important to be creative and get out of your comfort zone when it comes to studying technique. I do not like to perform the same studies over a long period of time; instead, I adjust my exercise routine according to the creative impulses and needs I feel at that moment.

I created these *16 Studies for Flamenco Guitar* to address the main flamenco guitar techniques in a more modern and inventive way, introducing new harmonies and minimizing the purely academic nature of most guitar exercises. You should perform these exercises daily to get the most out of this book. I recommend playing each exercise at three different speeds, starting very slow and increasing velocity incrementally without loss of precision or sound quality.

Without further ado, it's time to pick up your guitar and begin practicing these exercises! I hope you enjoy and benefit from playing them.

Yago Santos

Prologue

Intended as a sequel to *20 Flamenco Guitar Etudes*, the longer, more developed exercises in *16 Studies for Flamenco Guitar* further explore characteristic flamenco guitar techniques including: *picado, arpeggio, tremolo, horquilla,* the "chop," *ligado*, and the thumb/index *alzapua* among others. These intermediate-level studies are written in standard notation and guitar tablature with online audio and video included for ease of learning.

The pieces are designed and fingered pragmatically to enhance the student's overall understanding of flamenco technique and encourage the use of a broader range of studies in daily practice. Left and right-hand digitation is provided throughout, along with occasional circled string numbers which clarify passages intended to be played higher on the fretboard, or on certain strings for a specific musical effect.

This book is unique not only for its inclusion of the author's stellar online audio and video recordings, but also for insightful practice tips that vary according to the player's years of experience and level of development. If you're thinking "WOW!"— that is the appropriate response; this is flamenco instruction at its best.

About the Audio and Video

All studies are accompanied by online audio and video recordings for illustration purposes. The studies are recorded by Yago Santos at normal speed so the student can visualize their correct interpretation, using the scores as needed.

Pulgar Study I

Presto ♩=175

Music by YAGO SANTOS

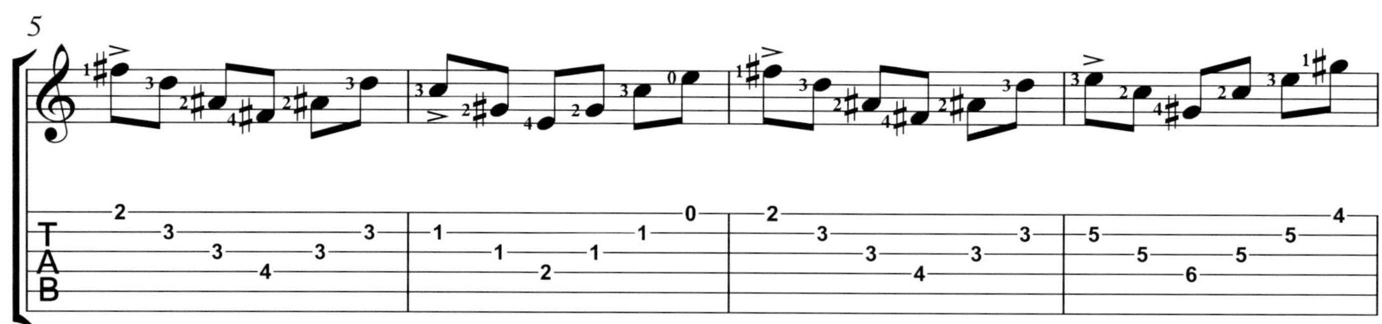

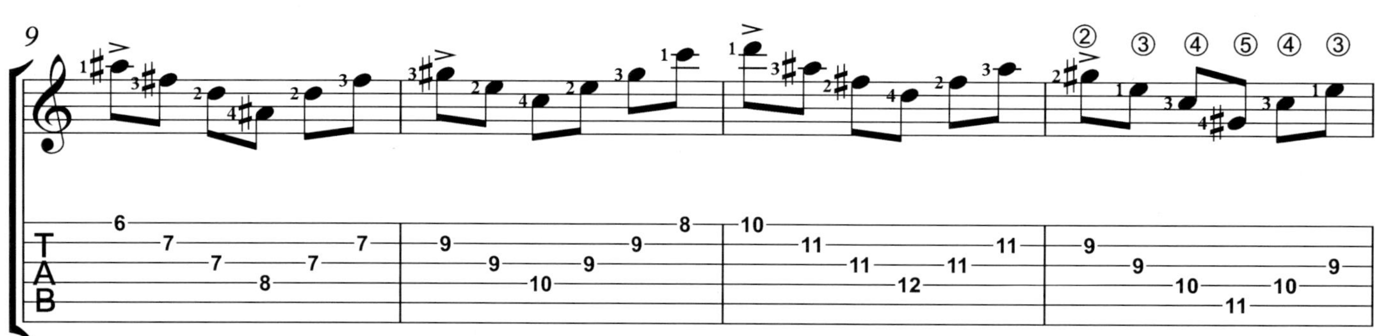

21
25
29
T
A
B

Picado Study I

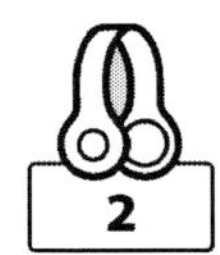

Picado = rest-stroke runs

Music by YAGO SANTOS

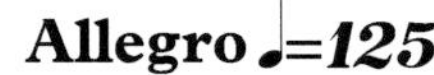

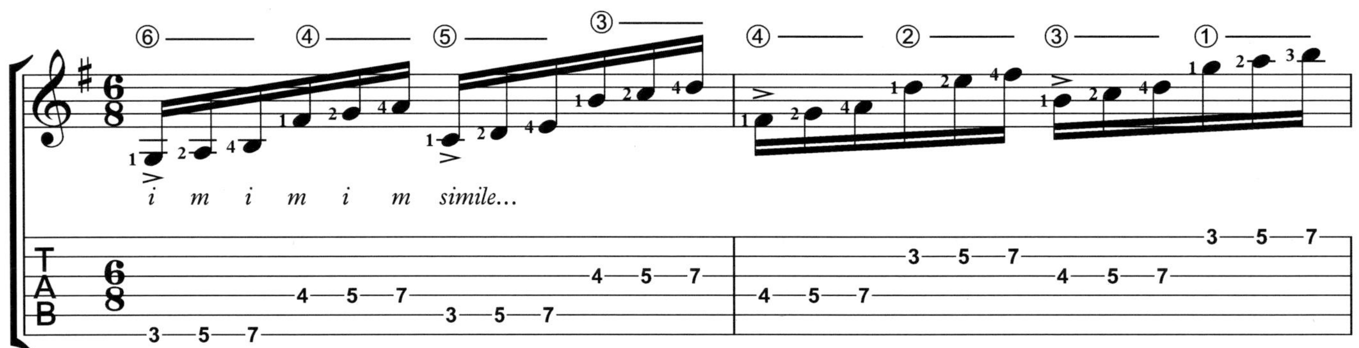

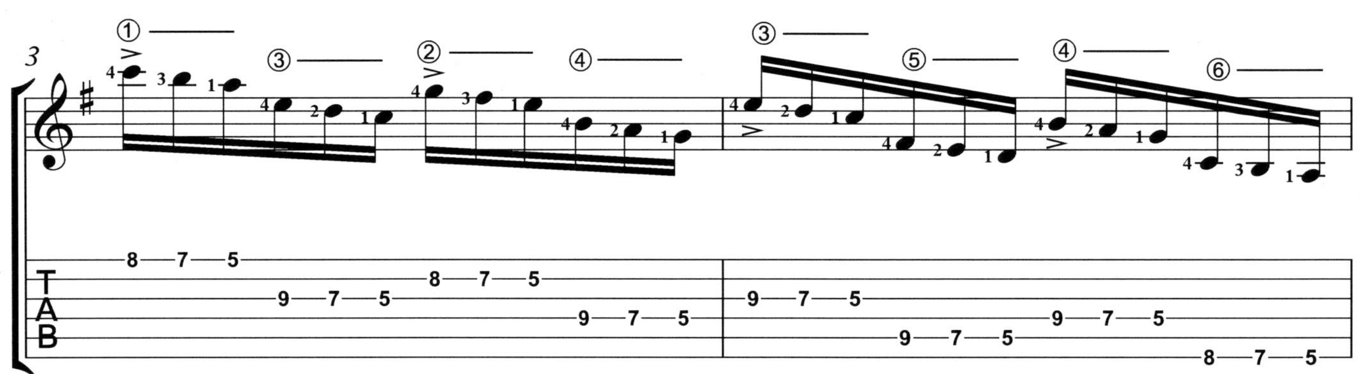

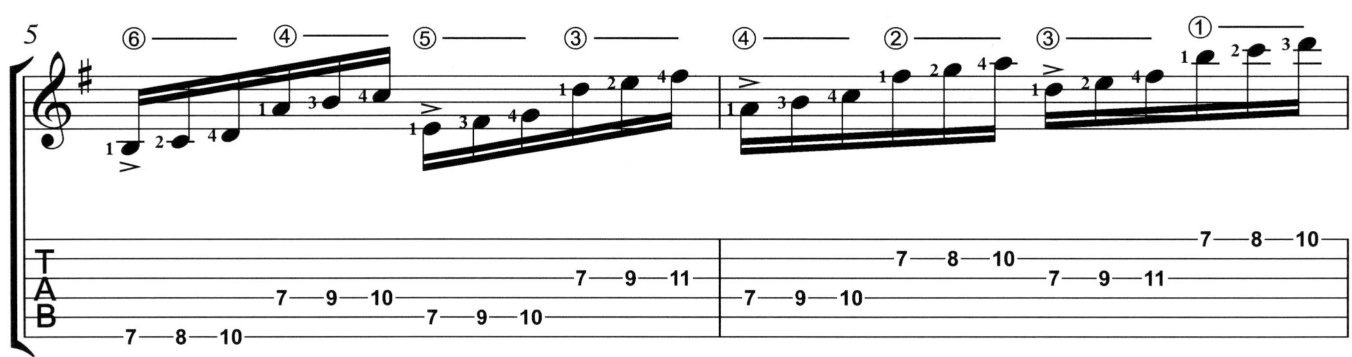

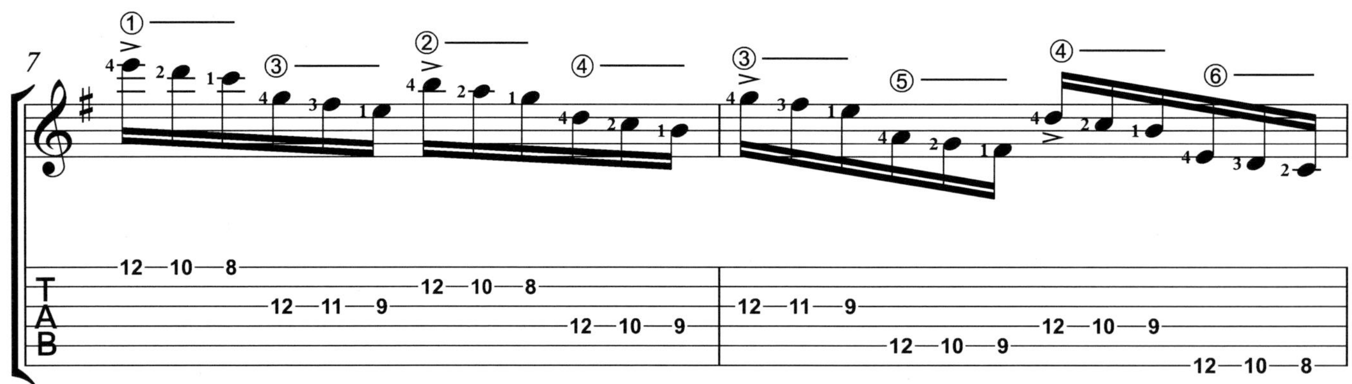

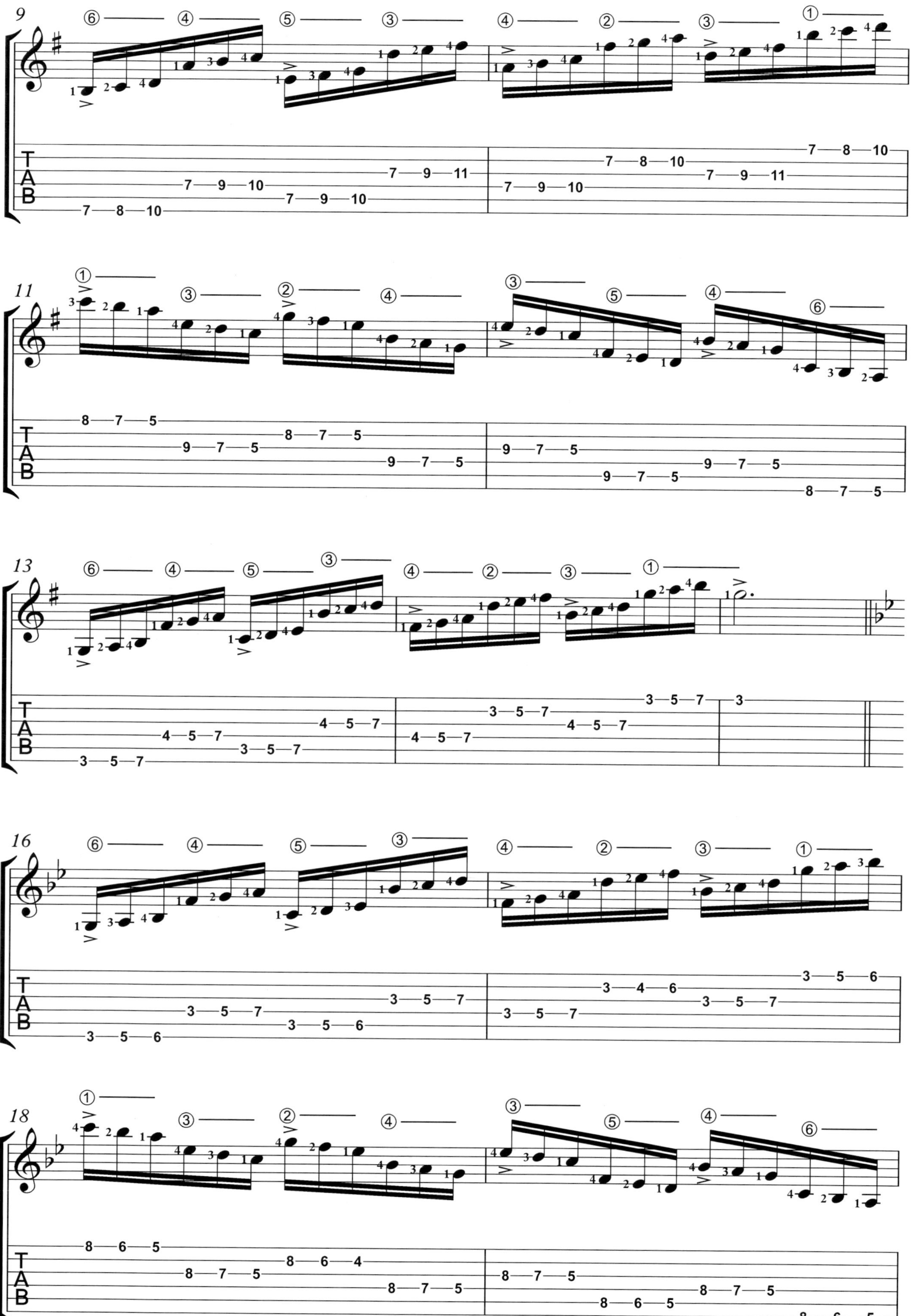

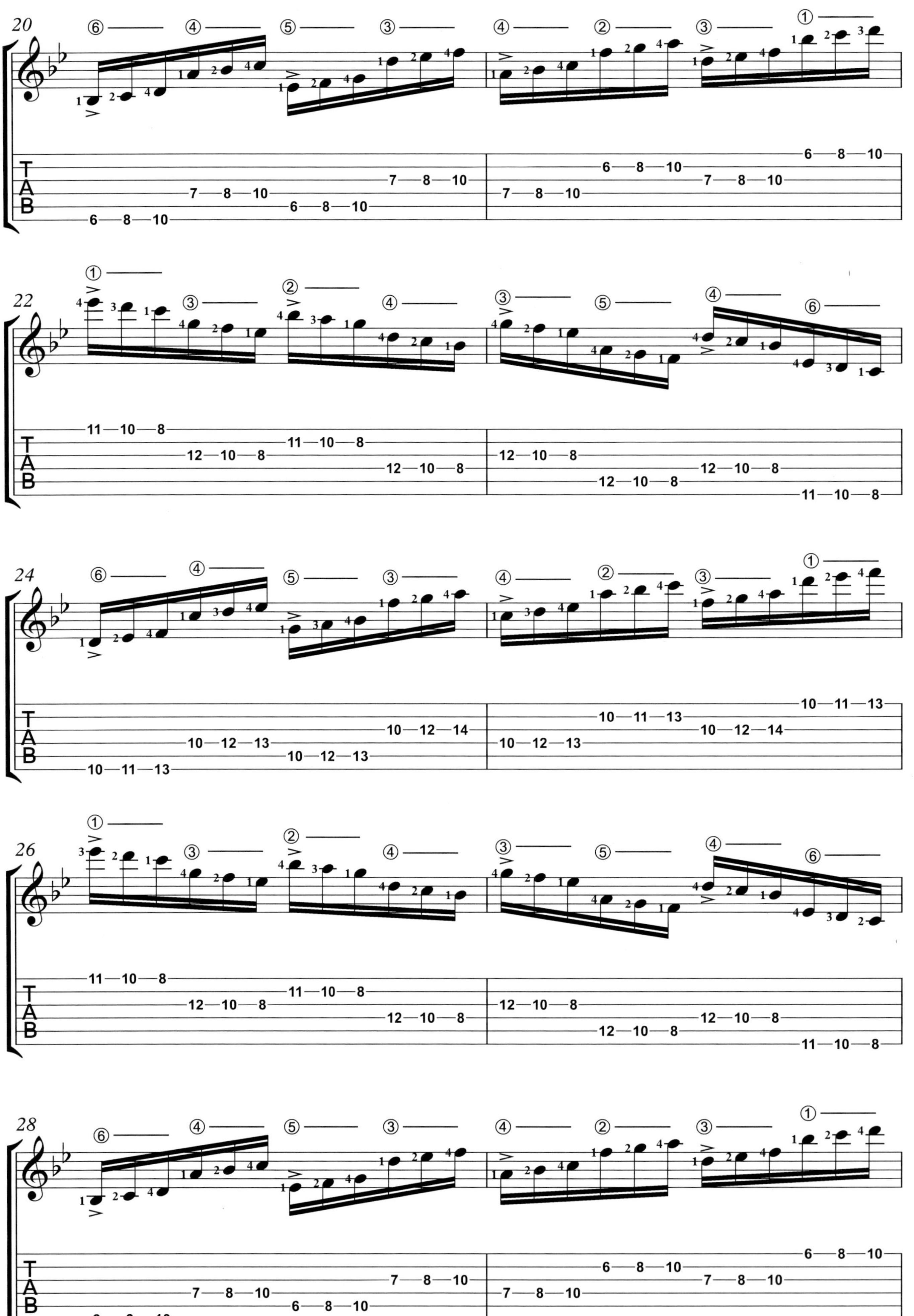

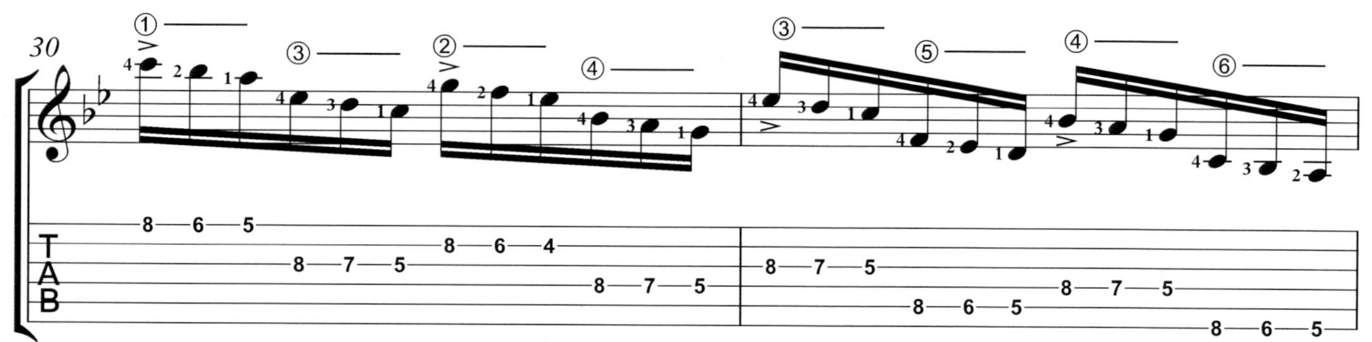
30
T
A
B

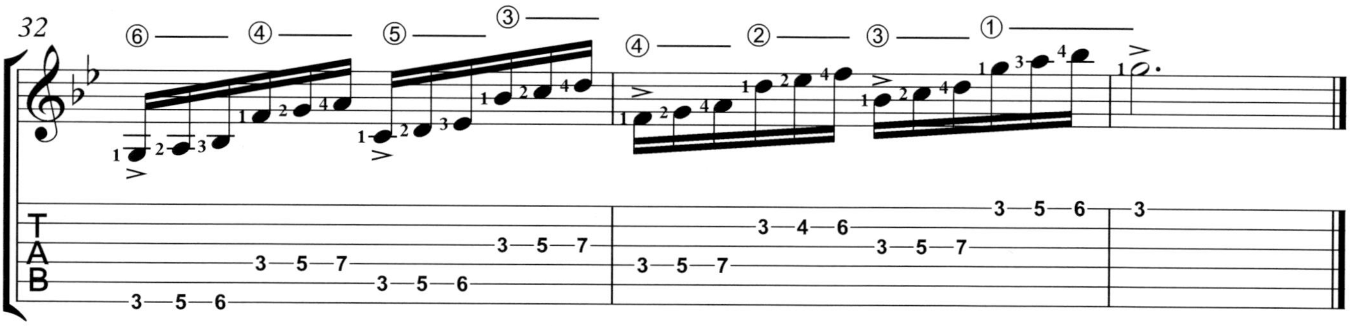
32
T
A
B

Horquilla Study

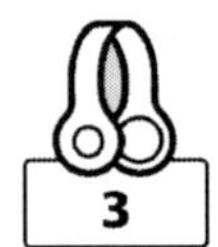

Horquilla refers to a triplet or septuplet rhythm played with a combination of thumb and fingers.

Music by YAGO SANTOS

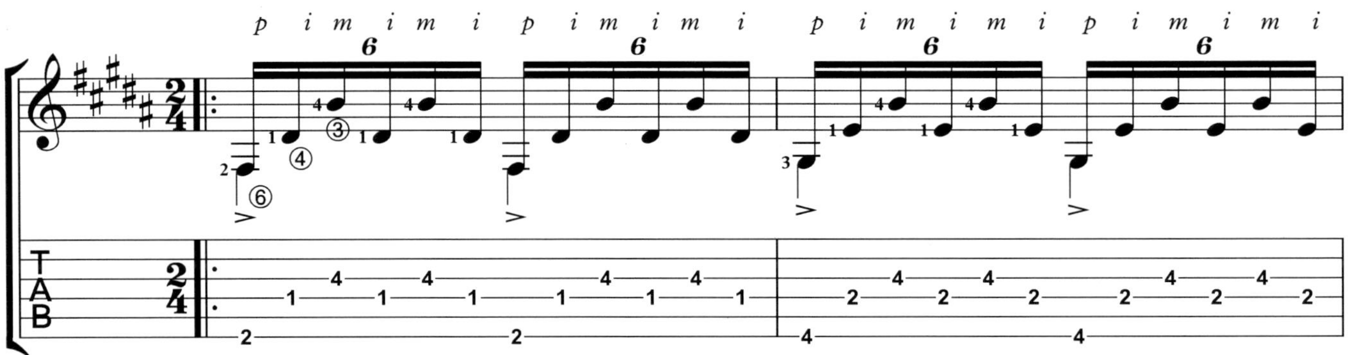

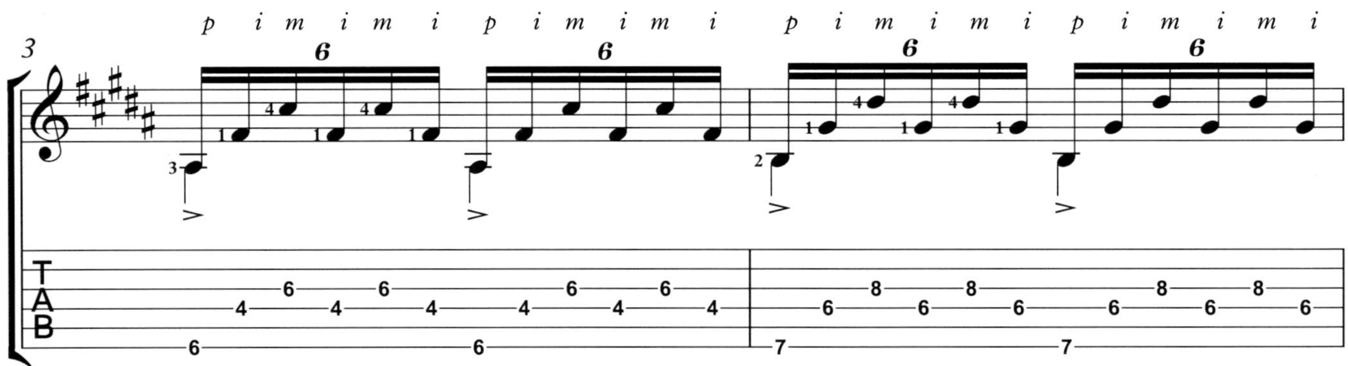

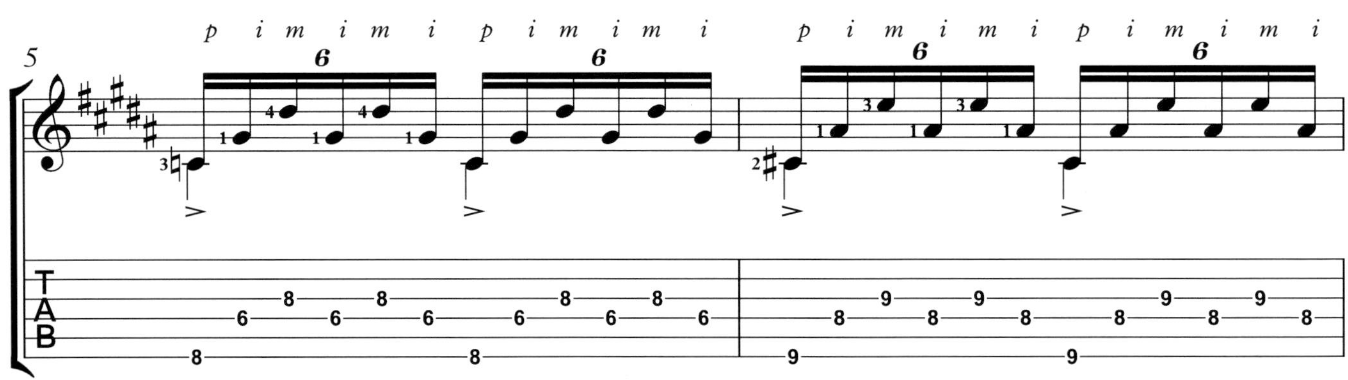

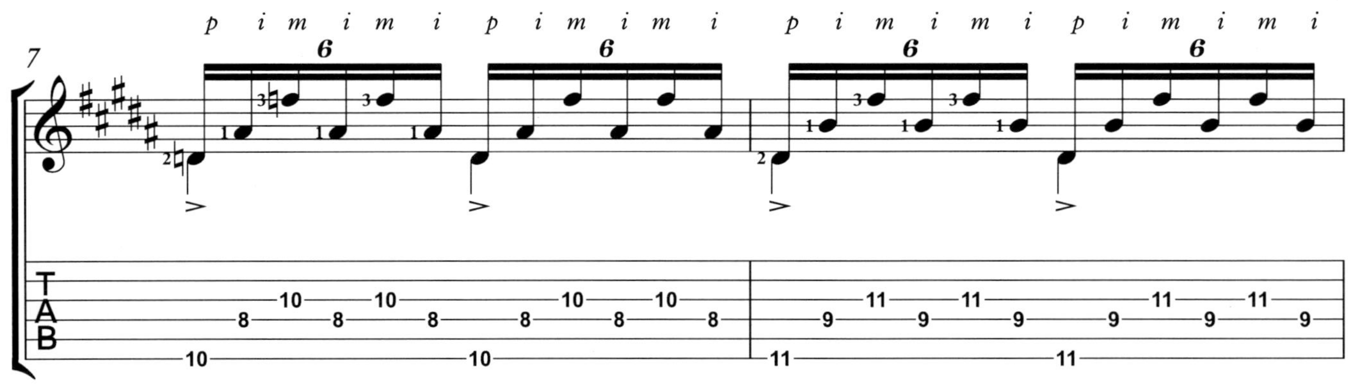

9
p i m i m i p i m i m i p i m i m i p i m i m i
11
p i m i m i p i m i m i p i m i m i p i m i m i
13
p i m i m i p i m i m i p i m i m i p i m i m i
15
p i a i a i p i a i a i p i a i a i p i a m i m
17
p i m p i a p i a p i m p i a p i a p i a p i a

19
p i a i a i p i a i a i p i a i a i p i a i a i
21
p i m i m i p i m i m i p i a i a i p i a m i m
23
p i m p i a p i a p i m p i a p i a p i a p i a
25
a m i a m i a m i a m i a m i a m i a m i a m i
27
a m i a m i a m i a m i a m i a m i m i m i m i

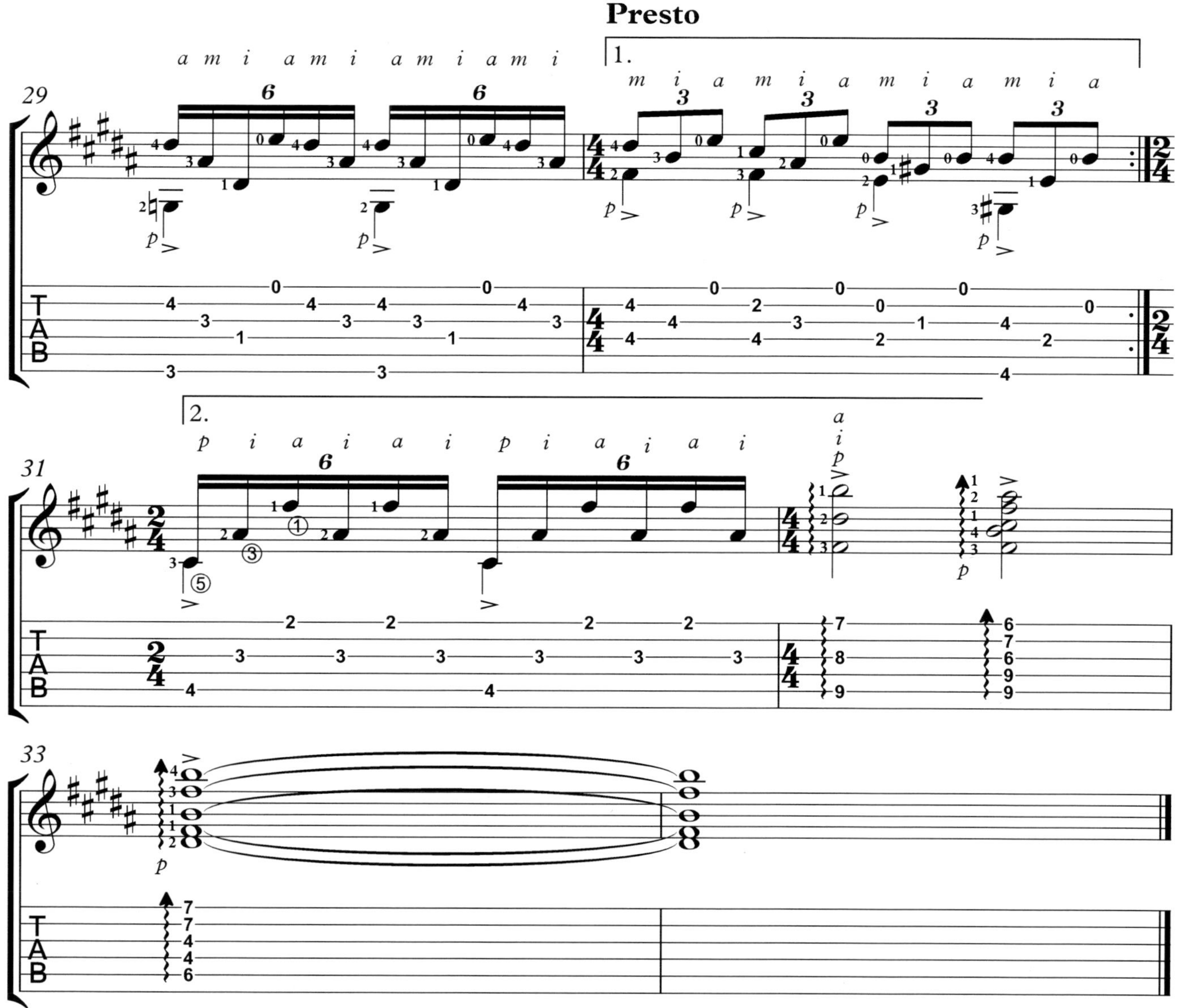
Presto
1.
2.
29
31
33

Picado Study II

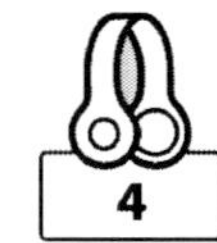

Music by YAGO SANTOS

Vivace ♩=*140*

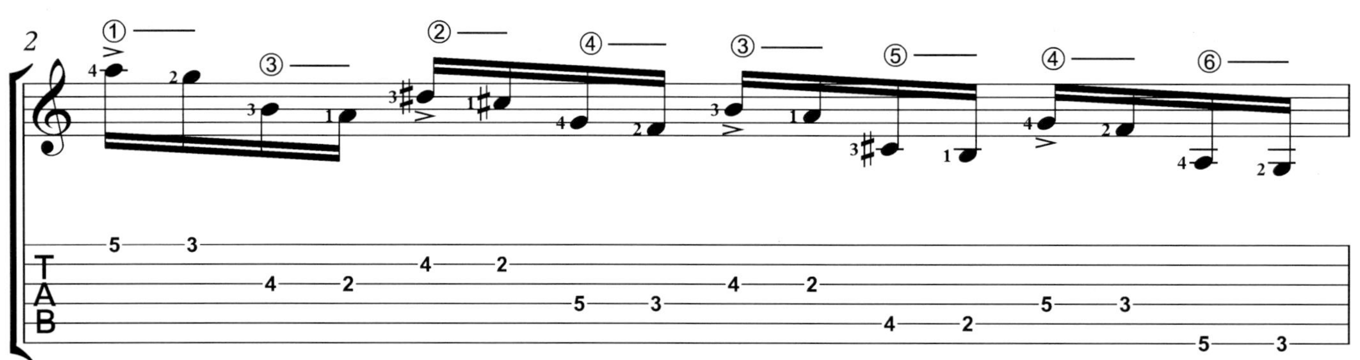

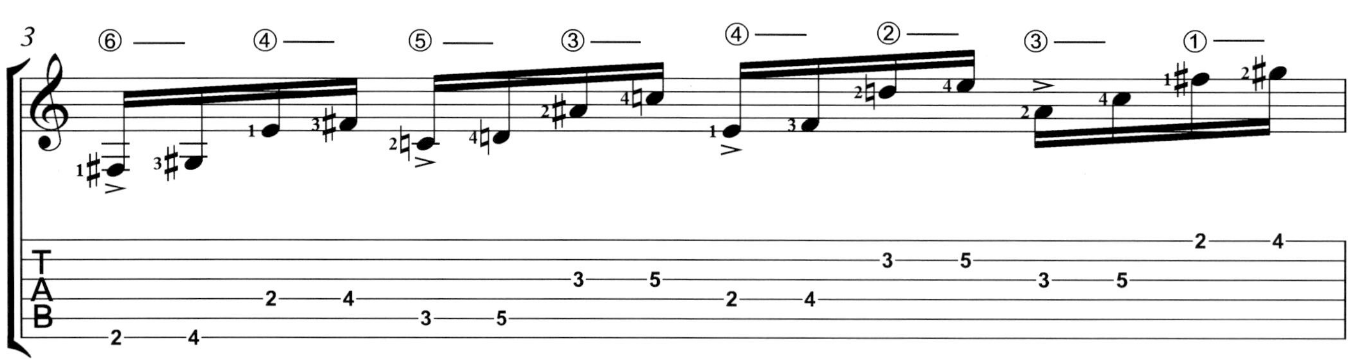

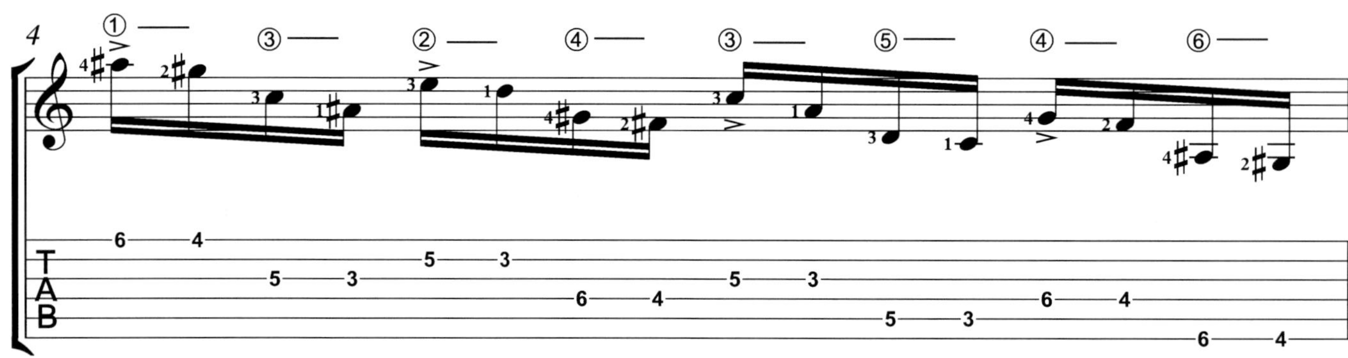

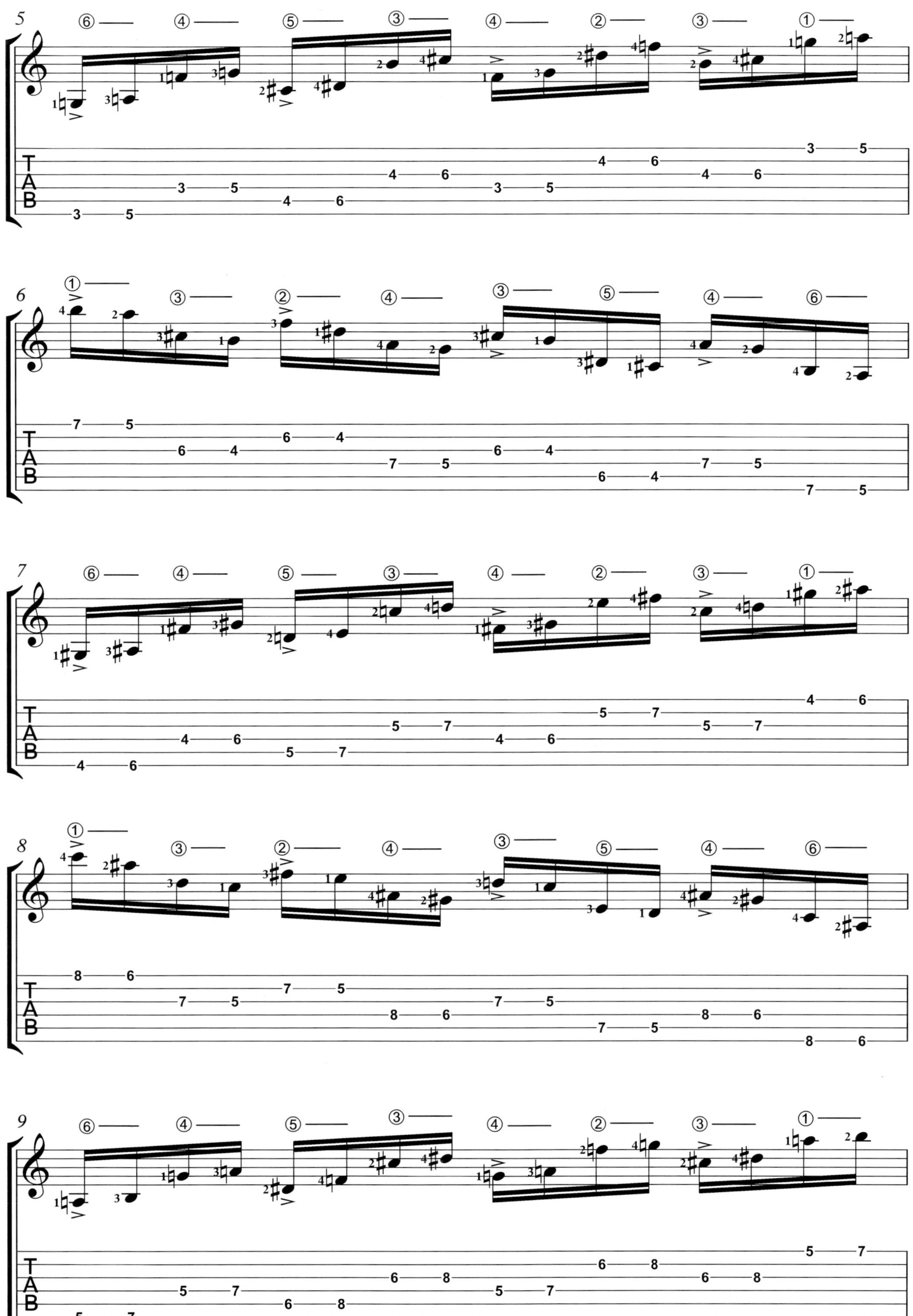

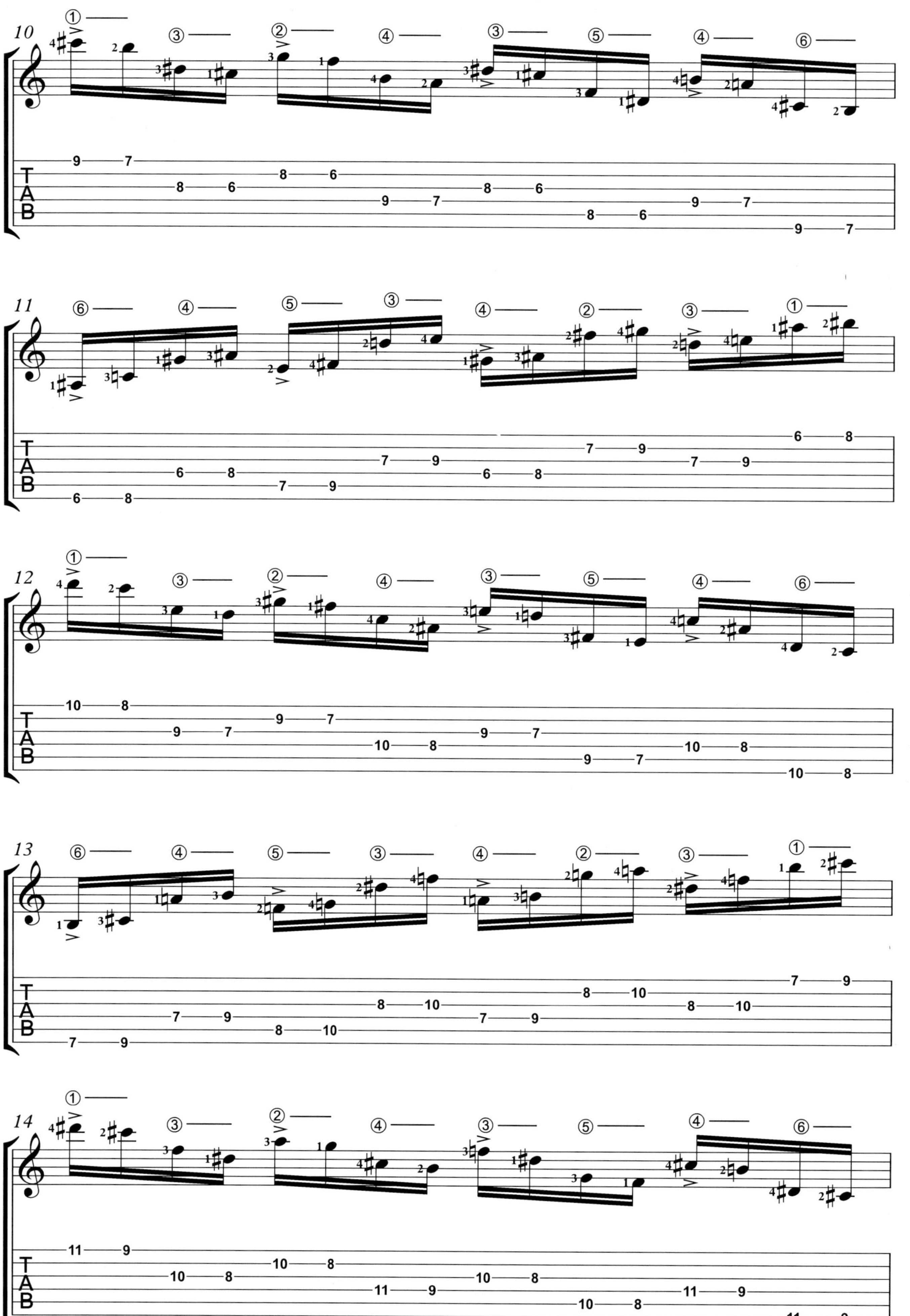

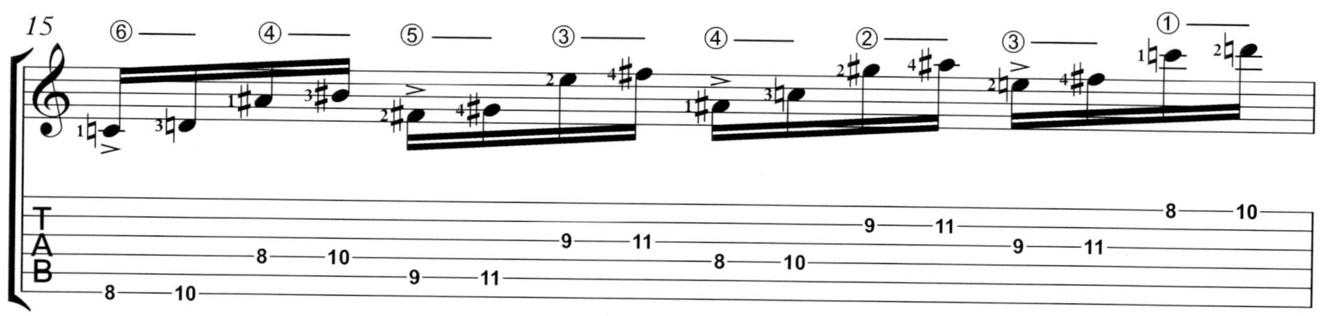
15
TAB

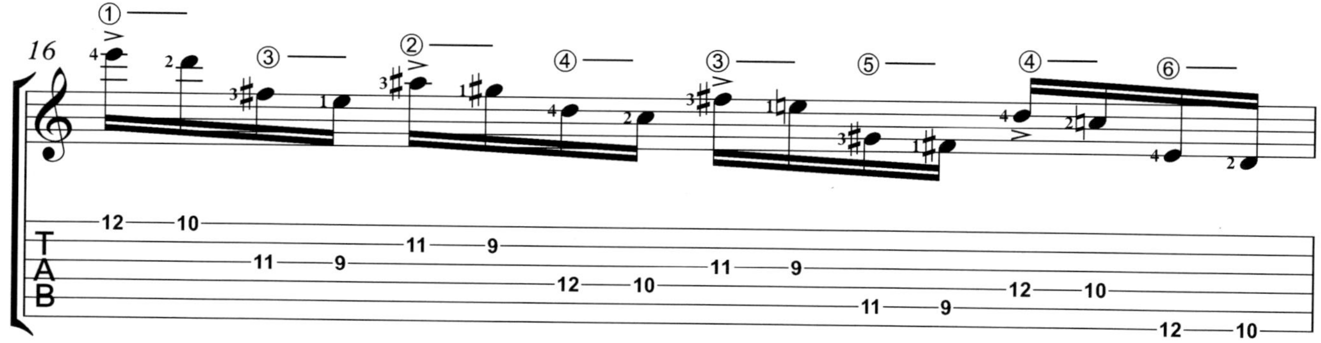
16
TAB

17
TAB

Chromatic Study I

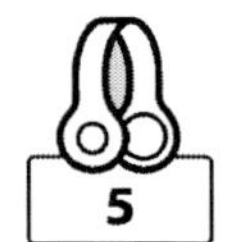

Music by YAGO SANTOS

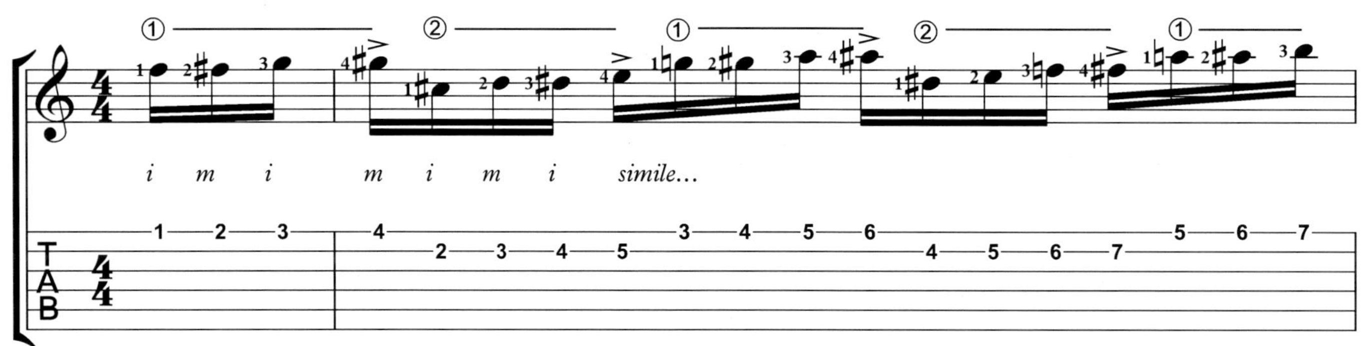

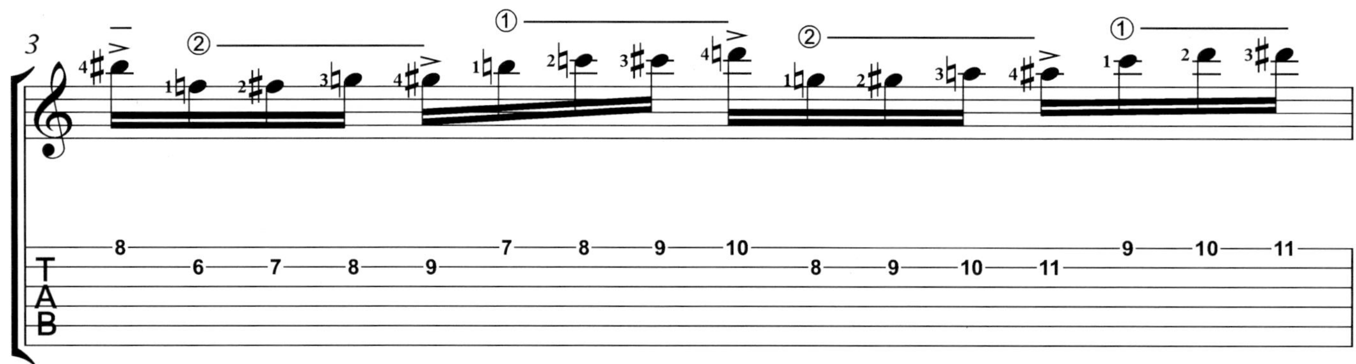

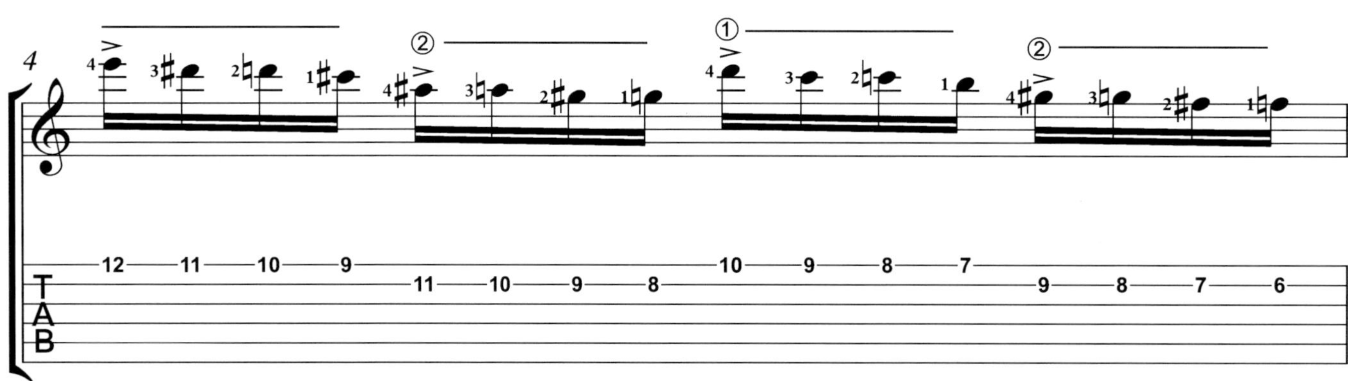

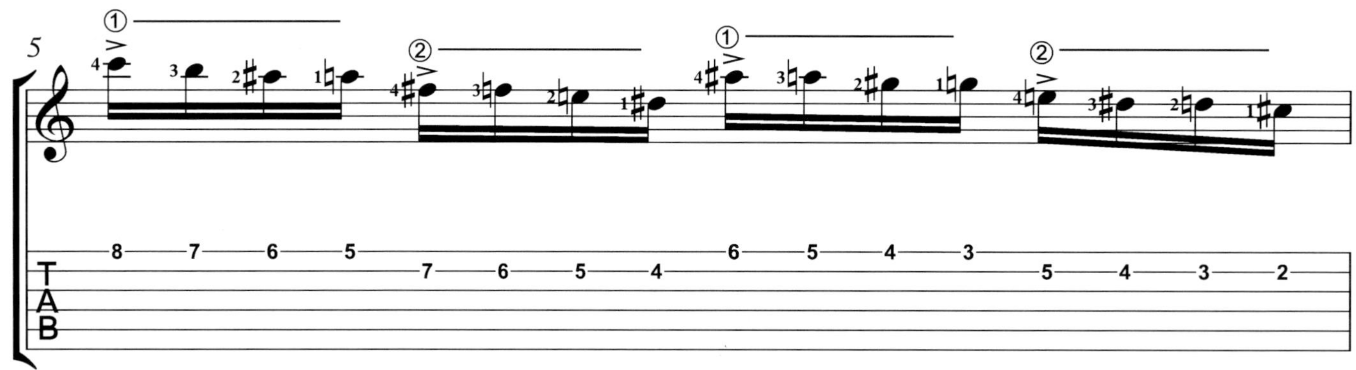

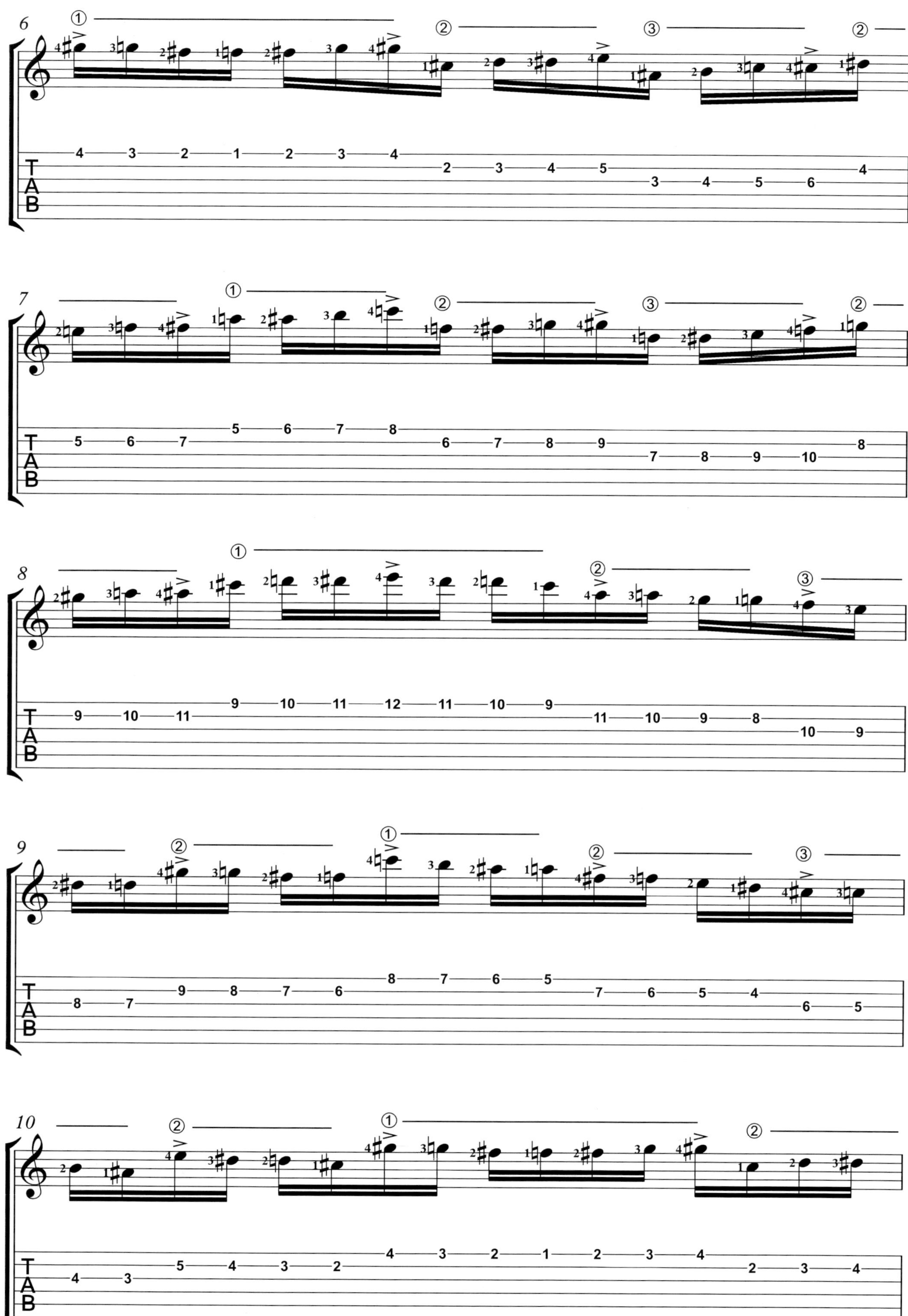

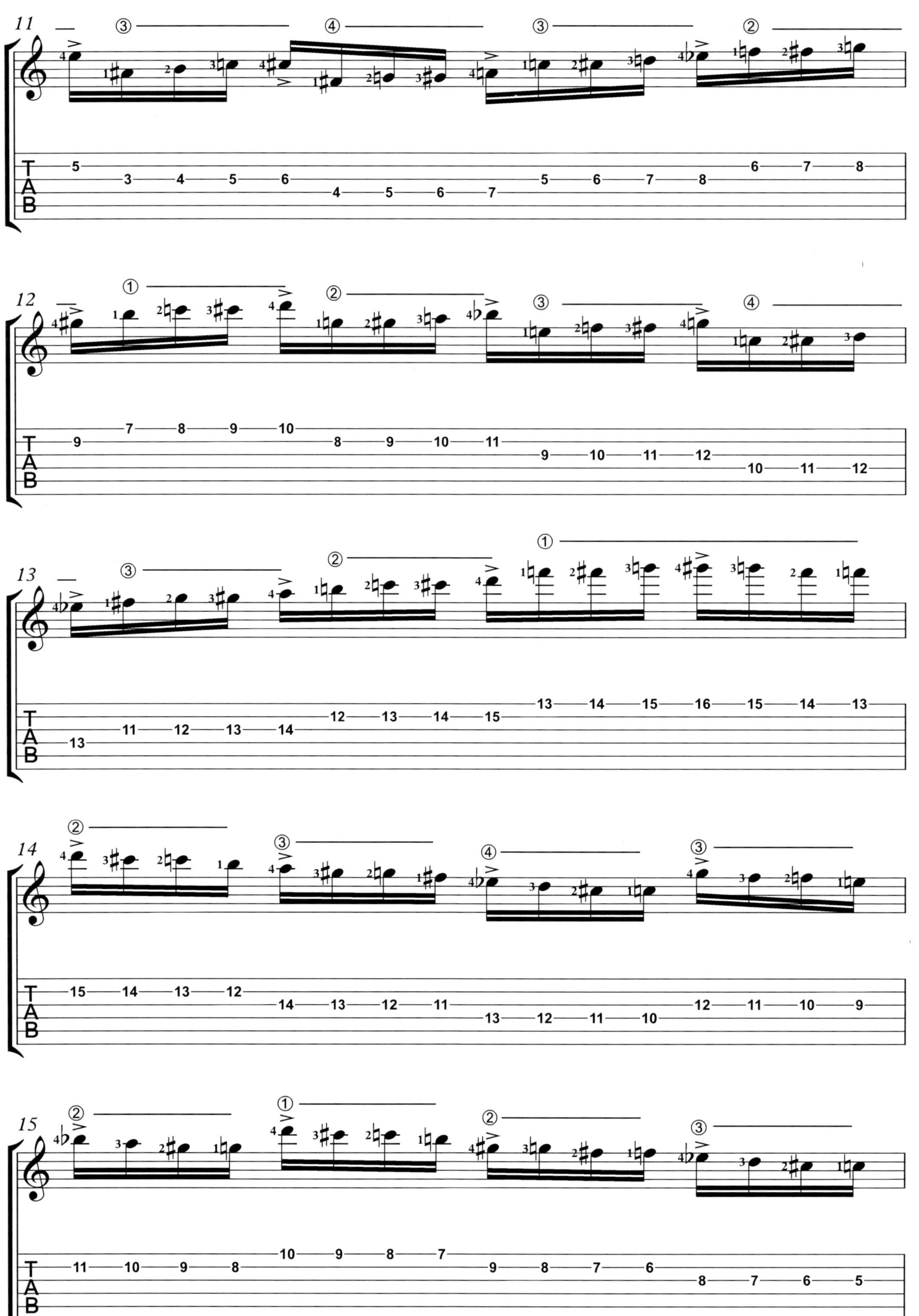

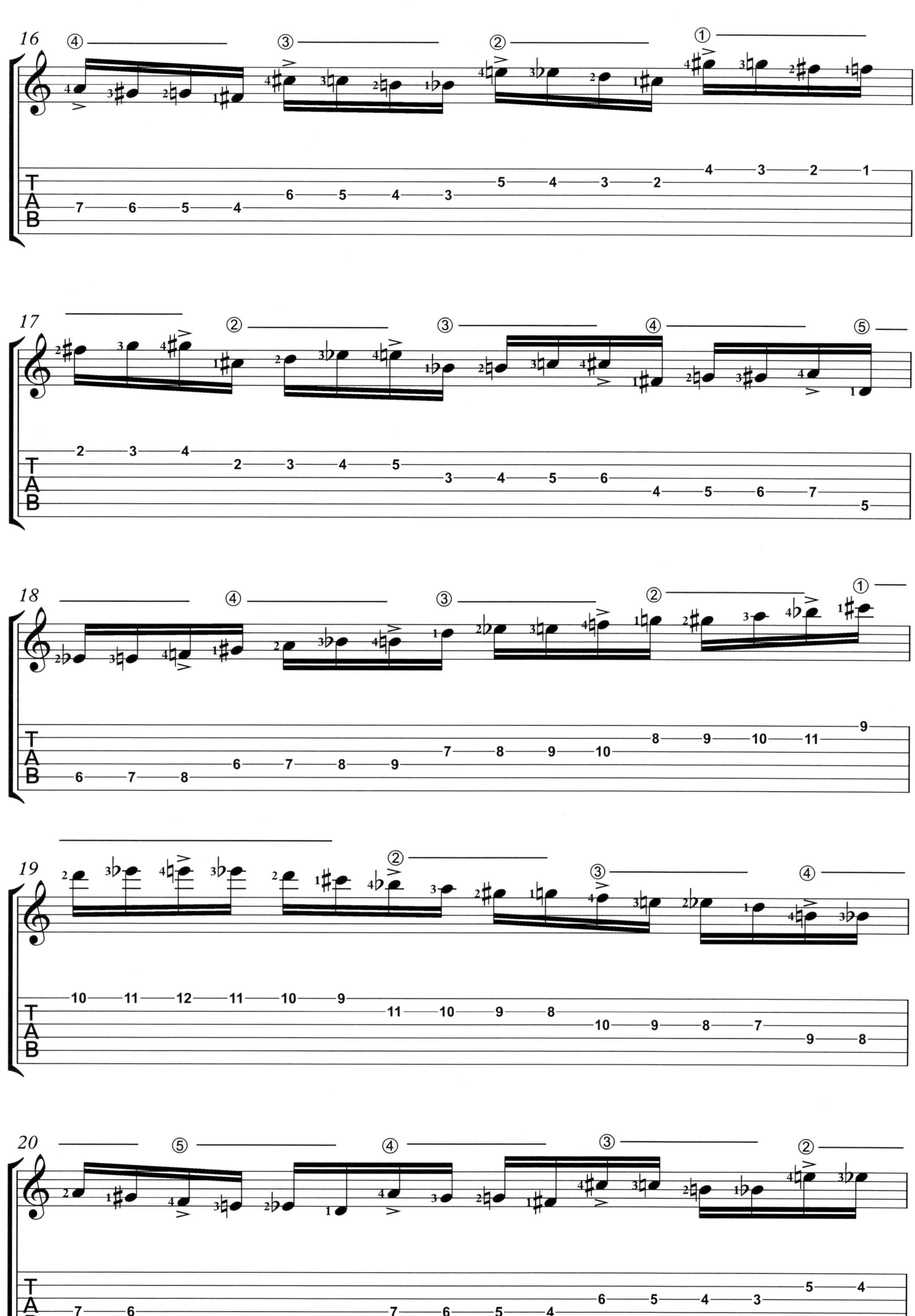

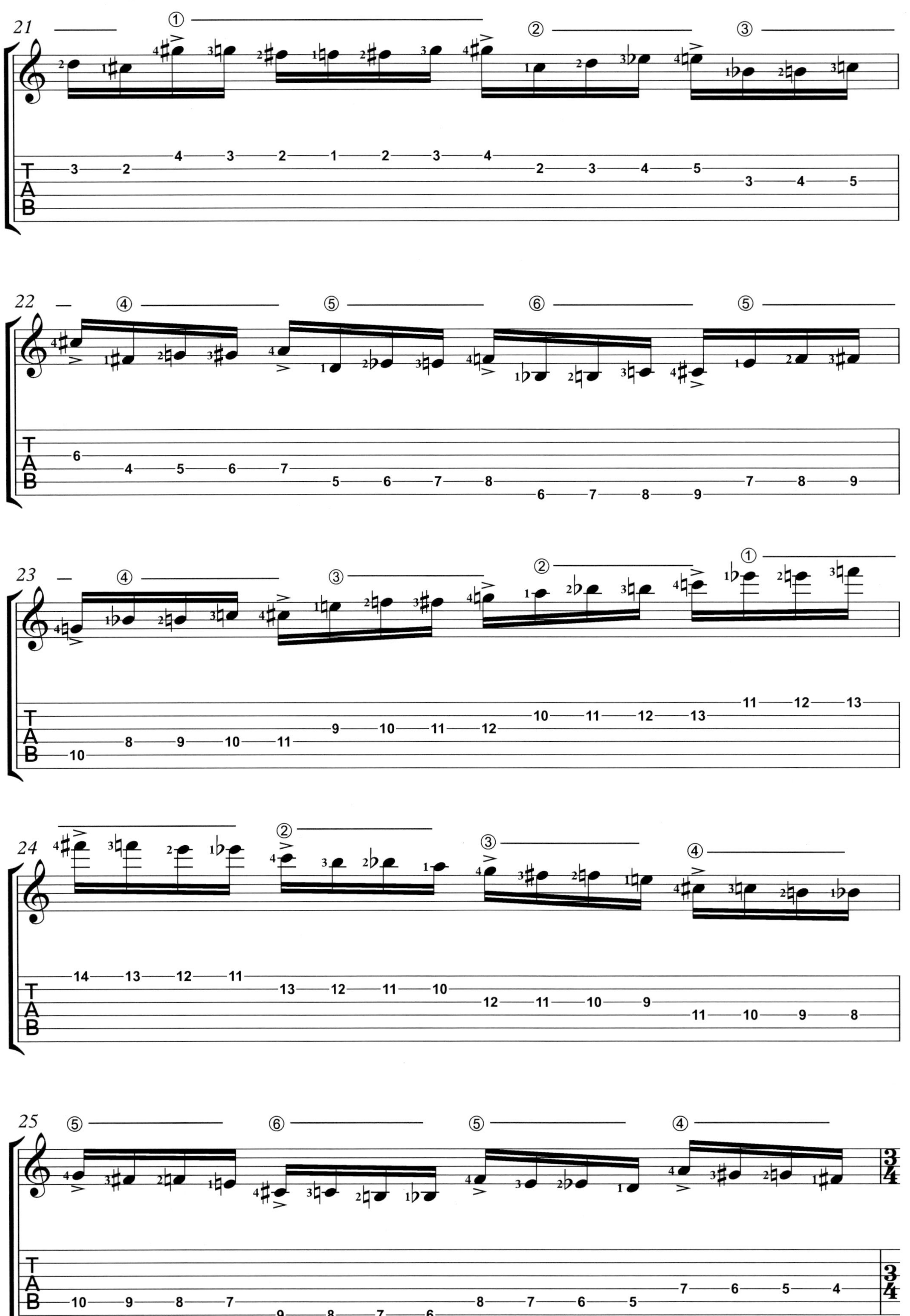

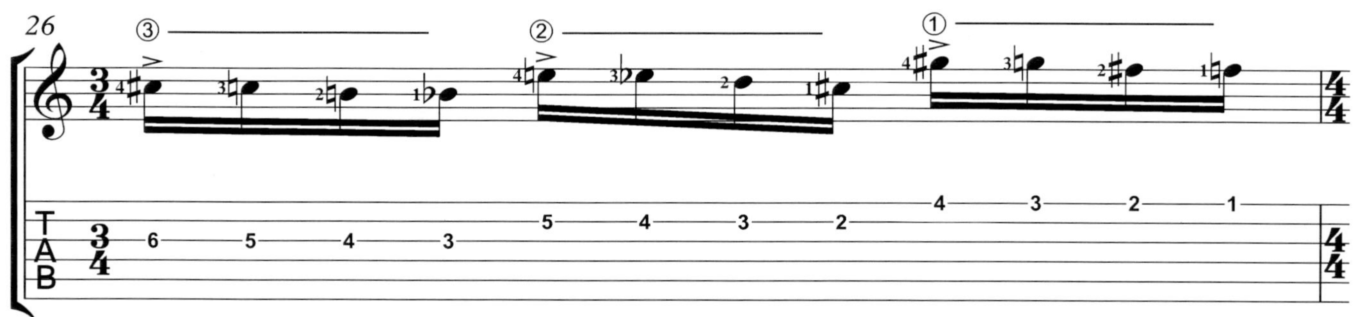
26
③
②
①
T
A
B
6
5
4
3
5
4
3
2
4
3
2
1

27
T
A
B
0

Chromatic Study II

Allegro ♩=120

Music by YAGO SANTOS

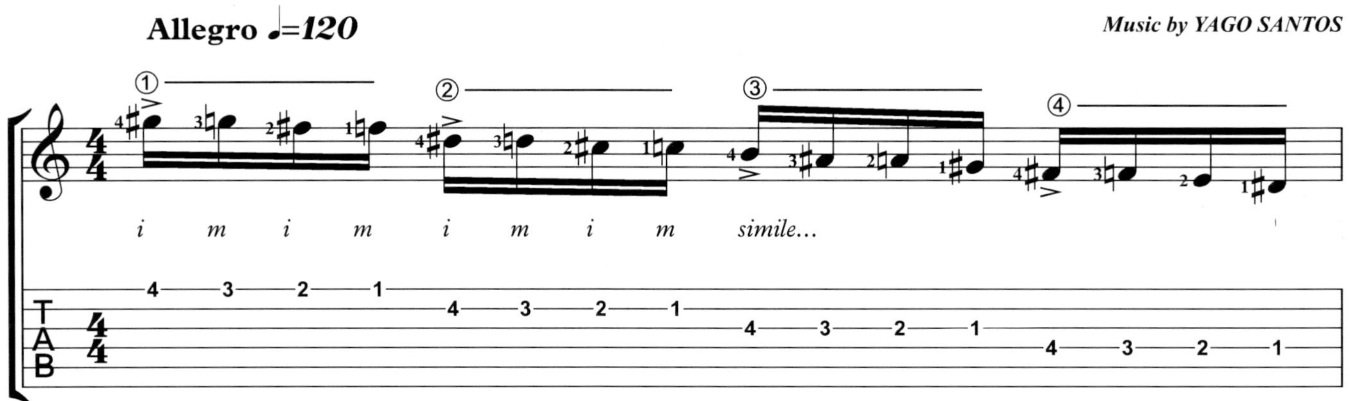

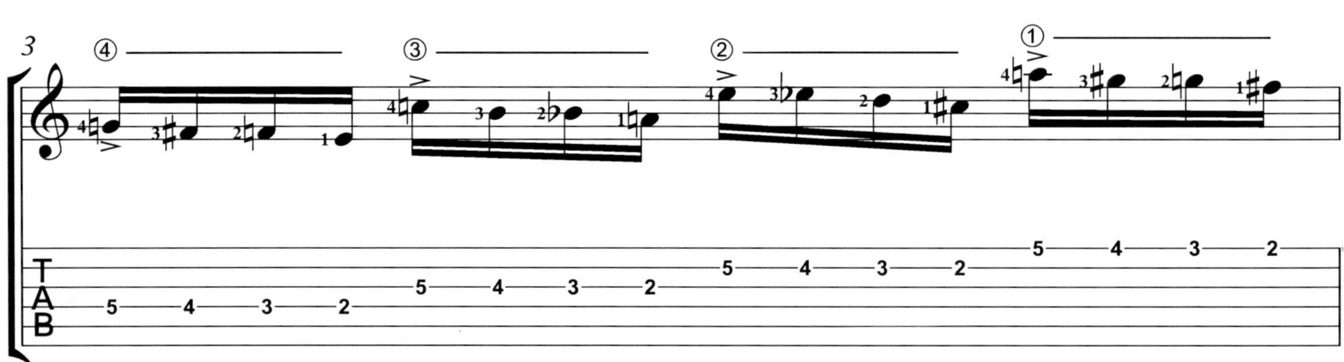

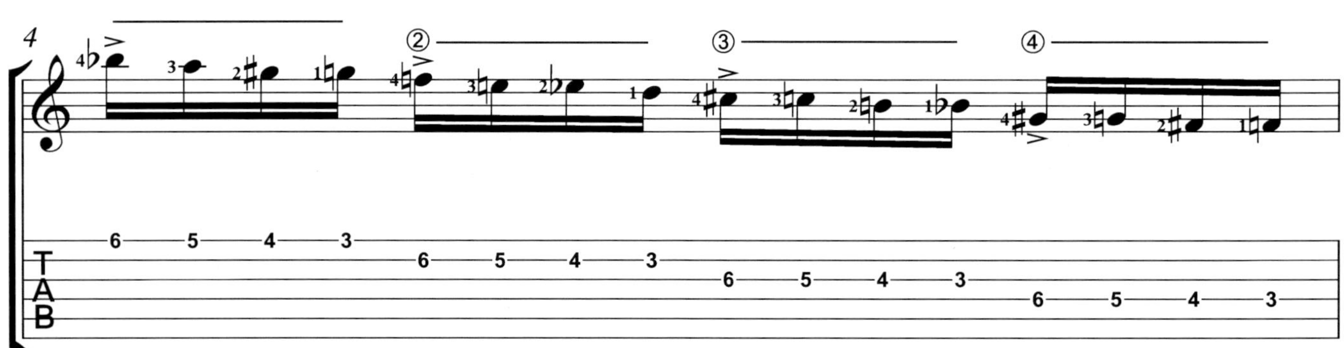

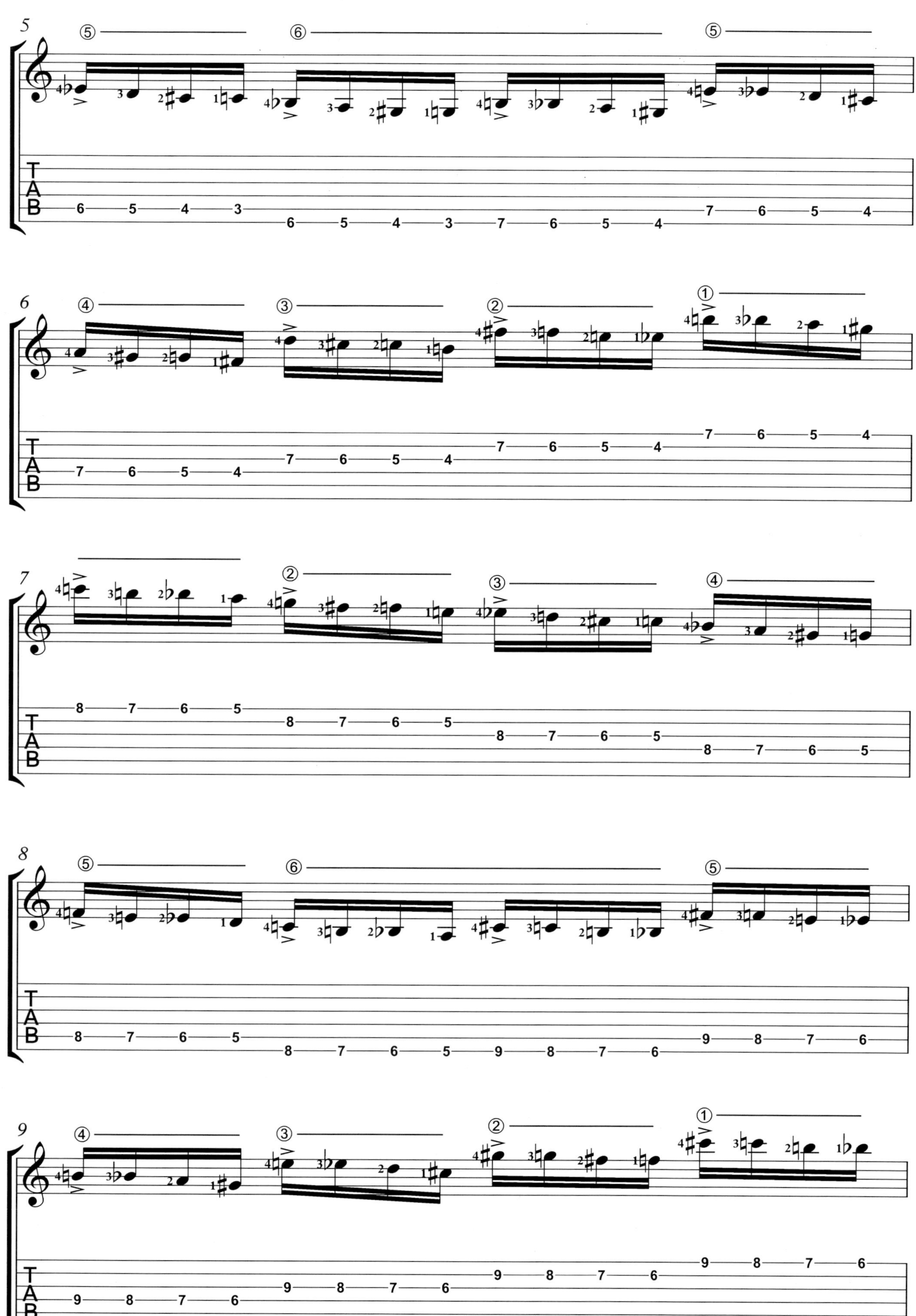

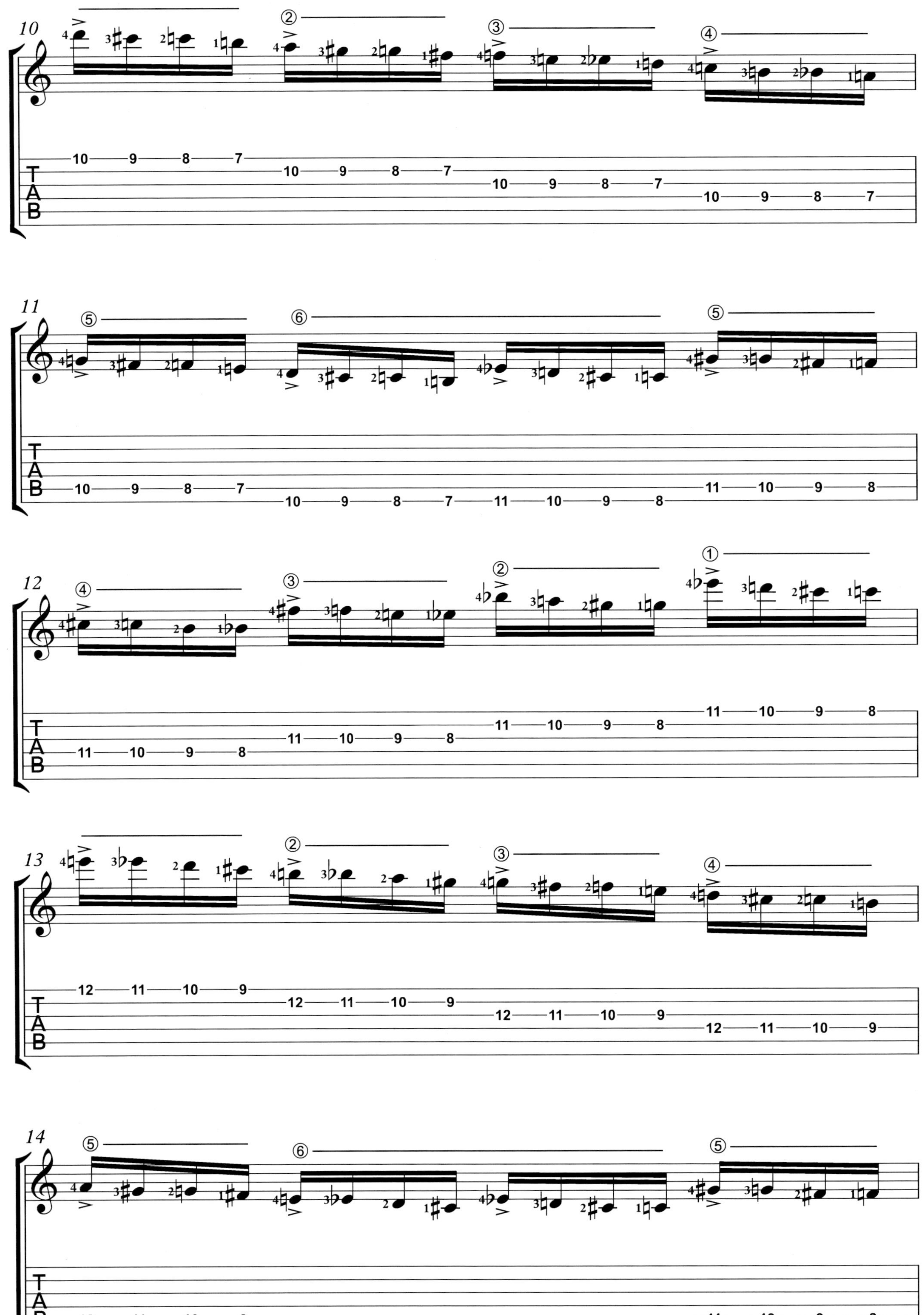

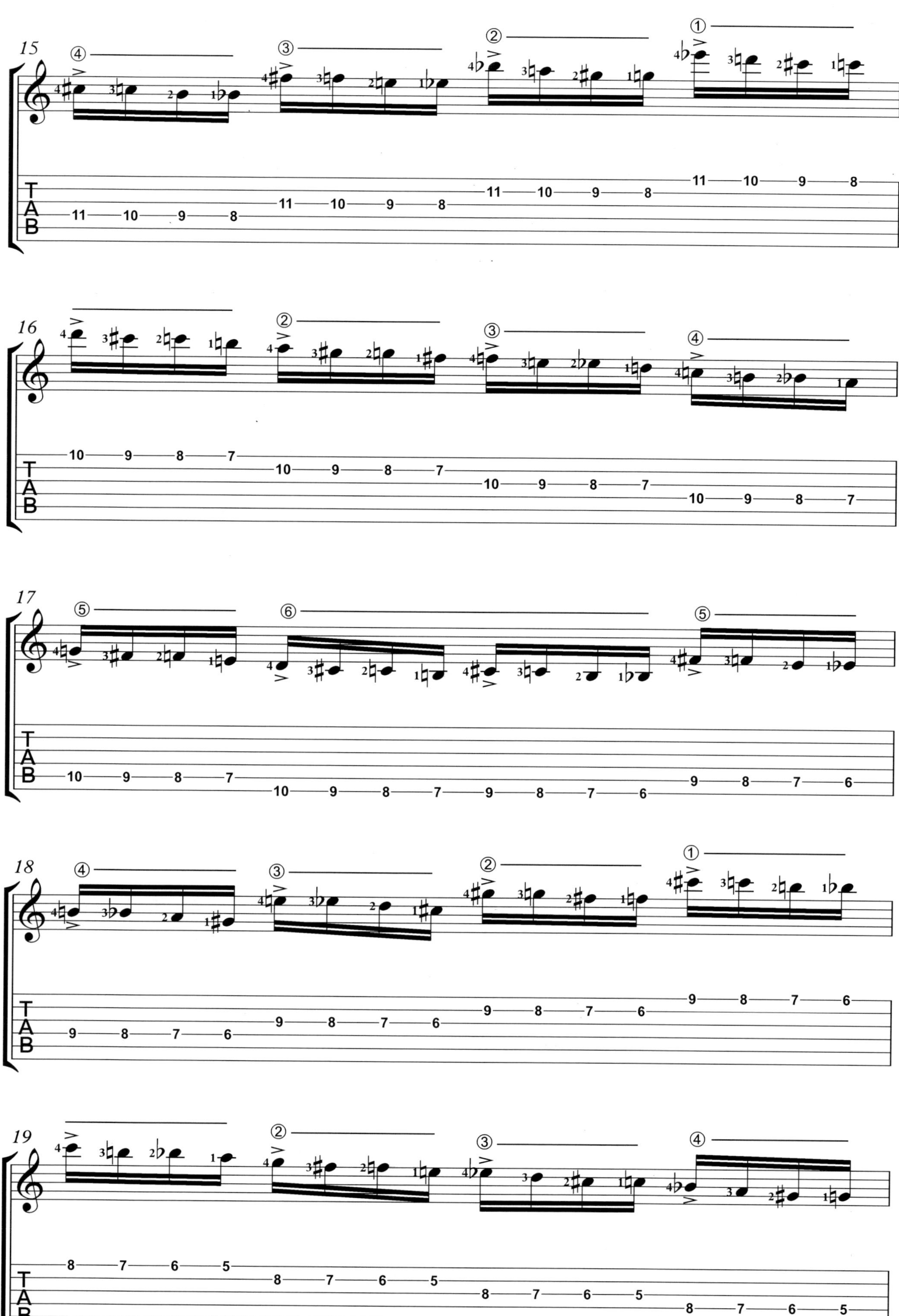

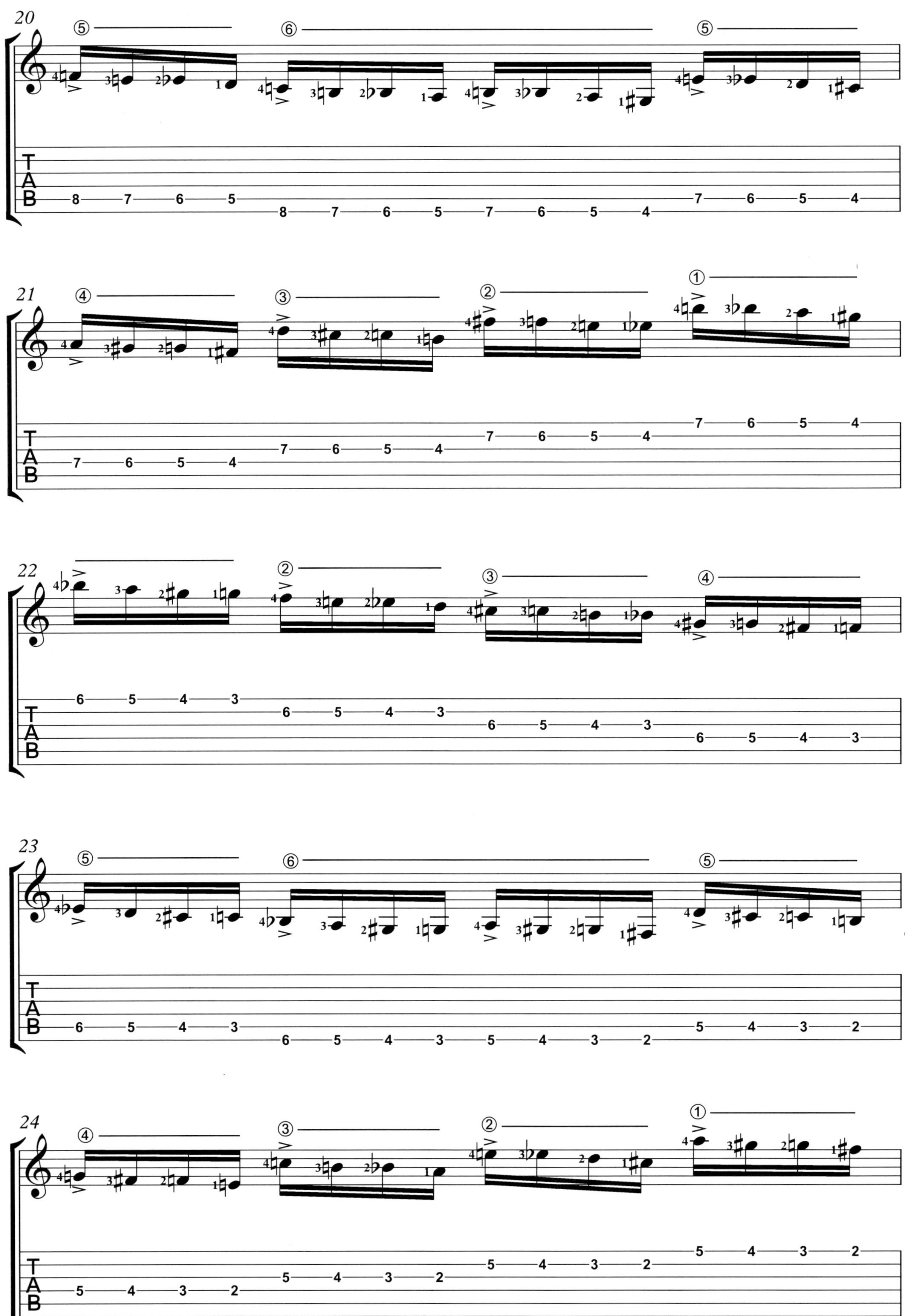
20
21
22
23
24
TAB

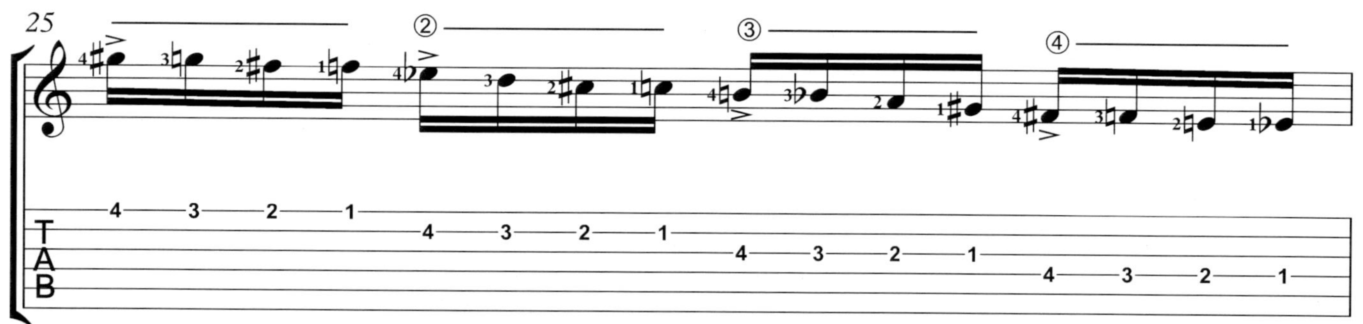

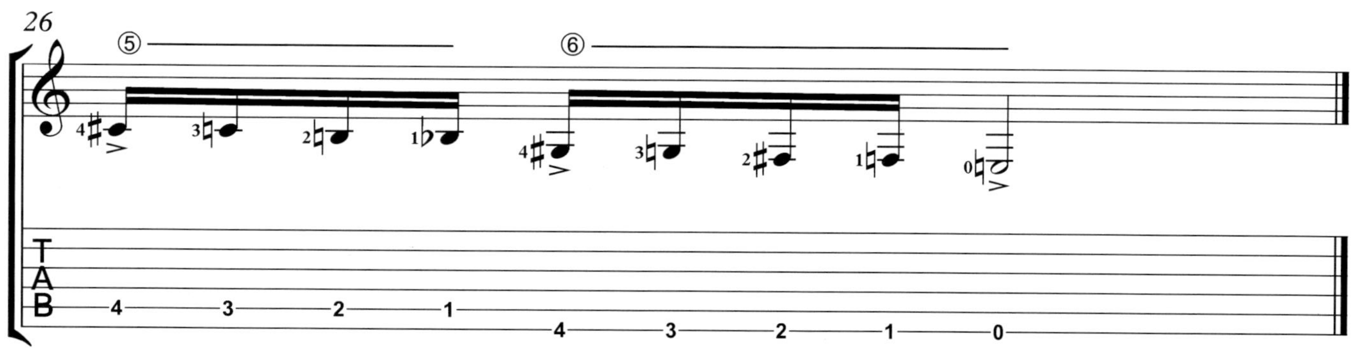

Picado Study III

Music by YAGO SANTOS

Allegretto ♩=*100*

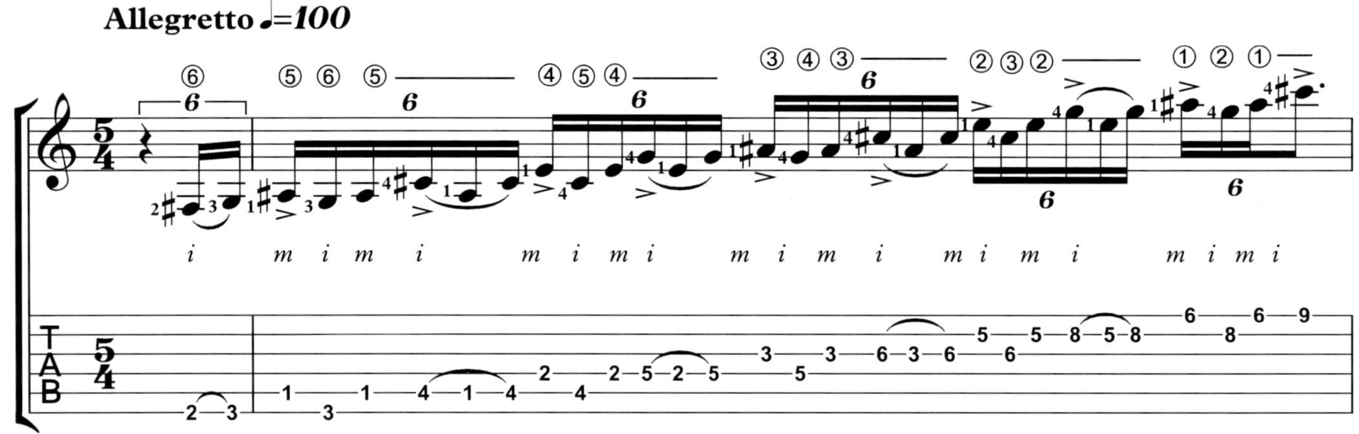

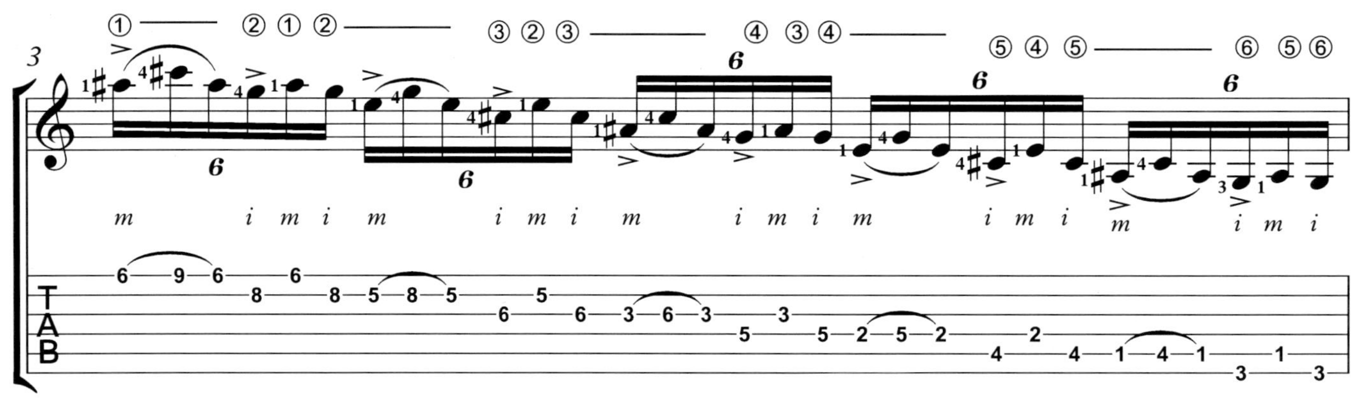

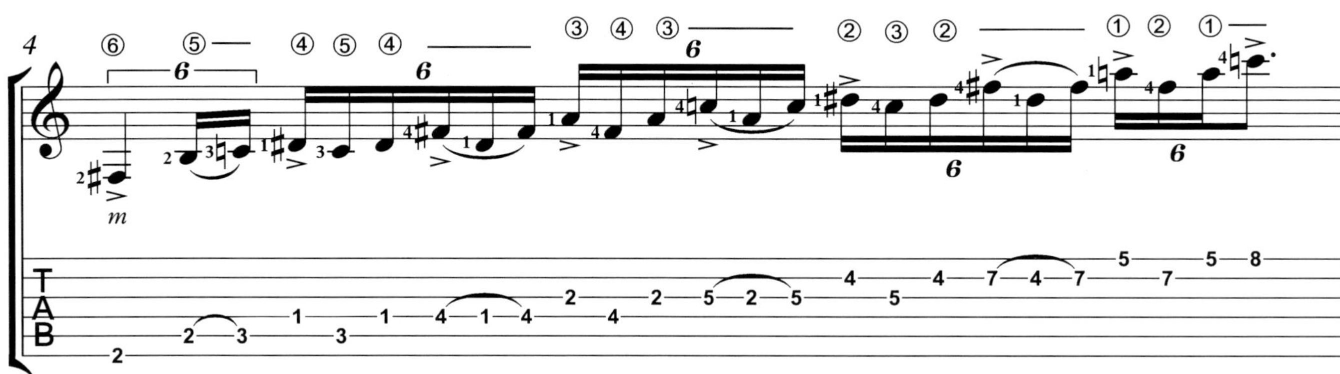

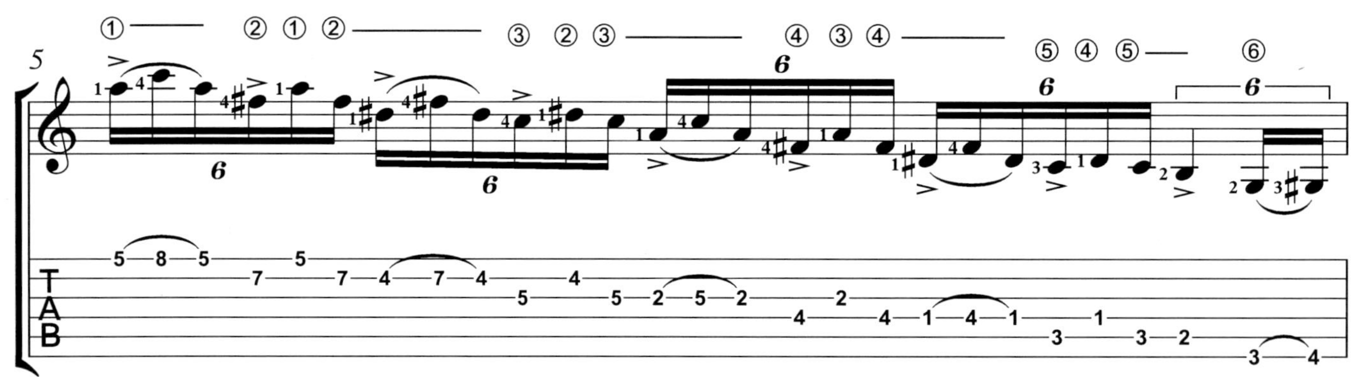

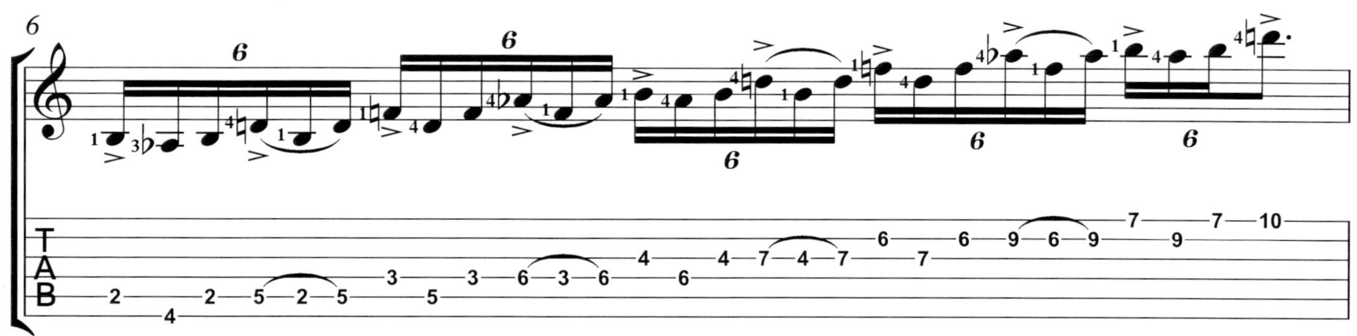

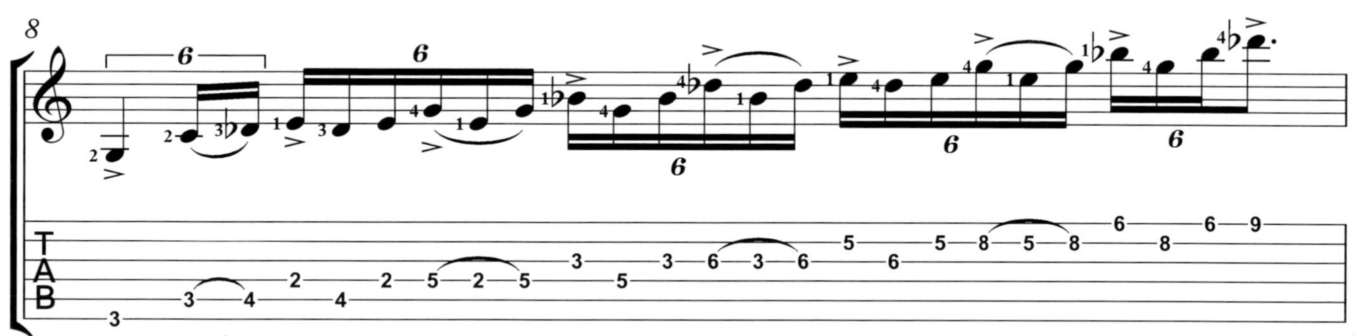
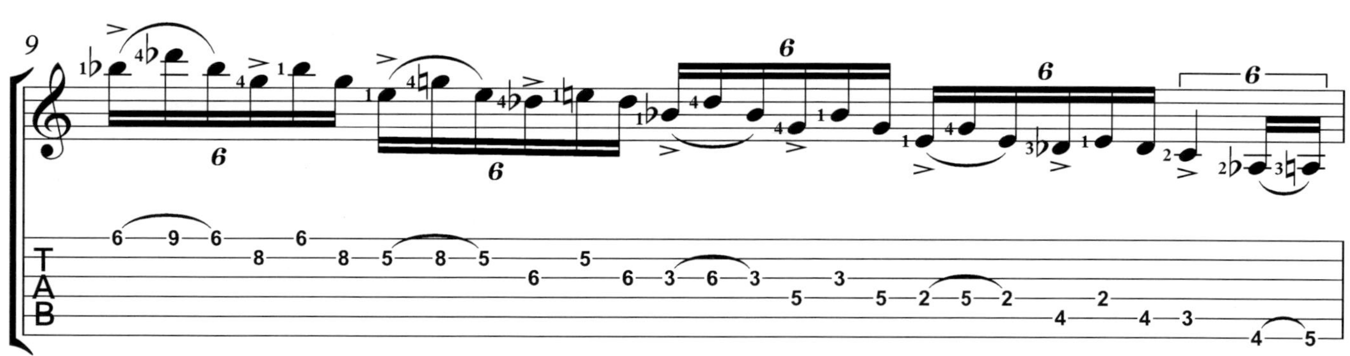
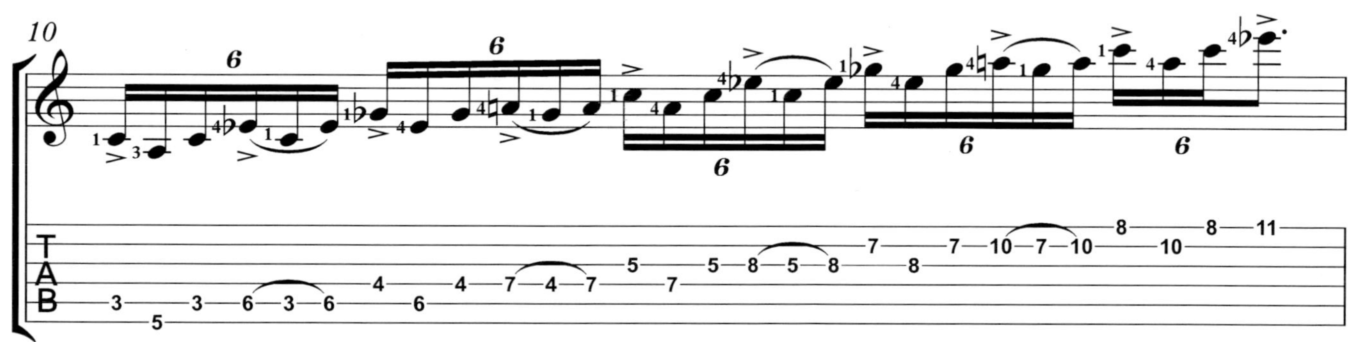

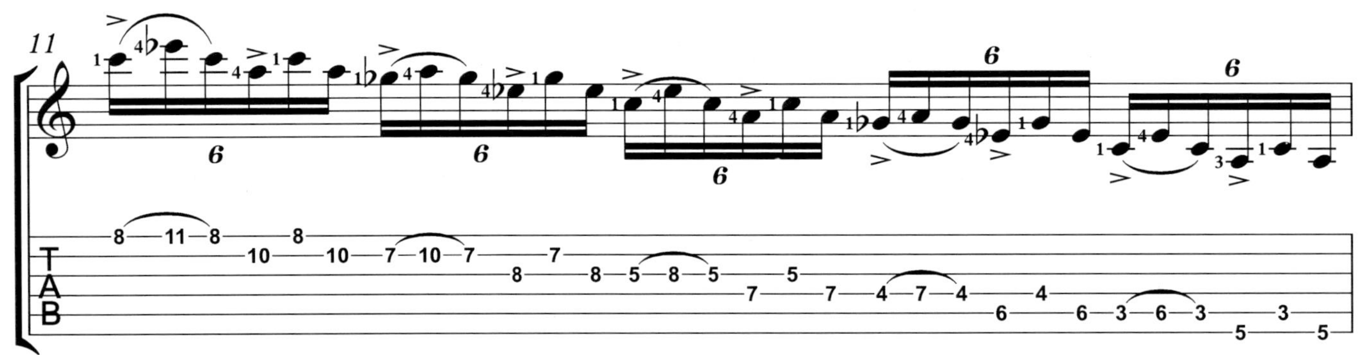
11
TAB

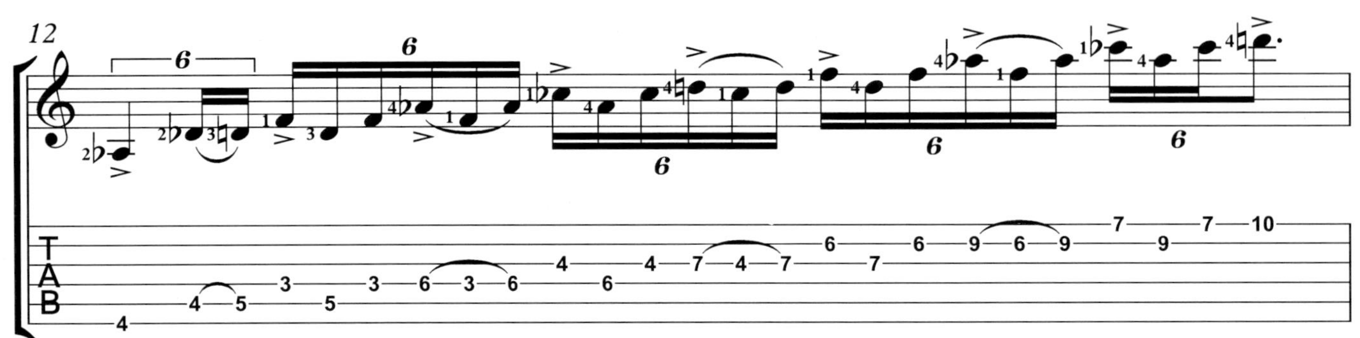
12
TAB

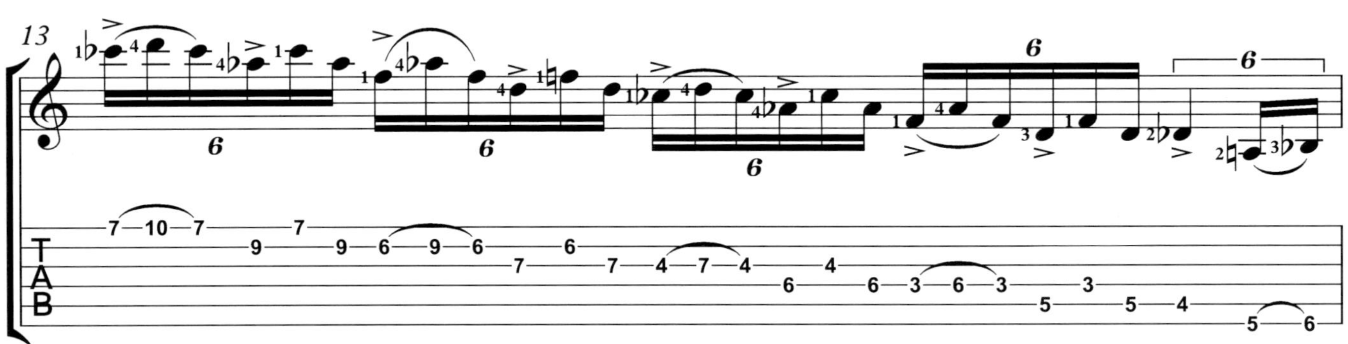
13
TAB

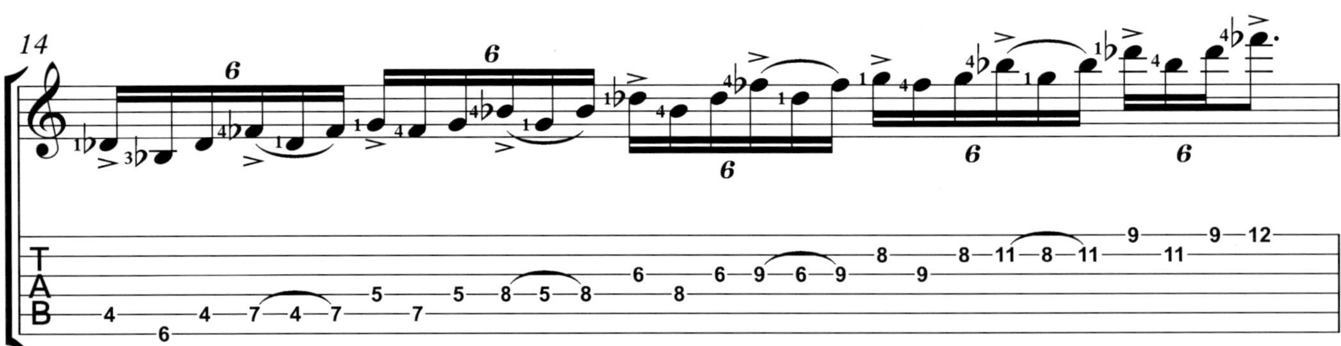
14
TAB

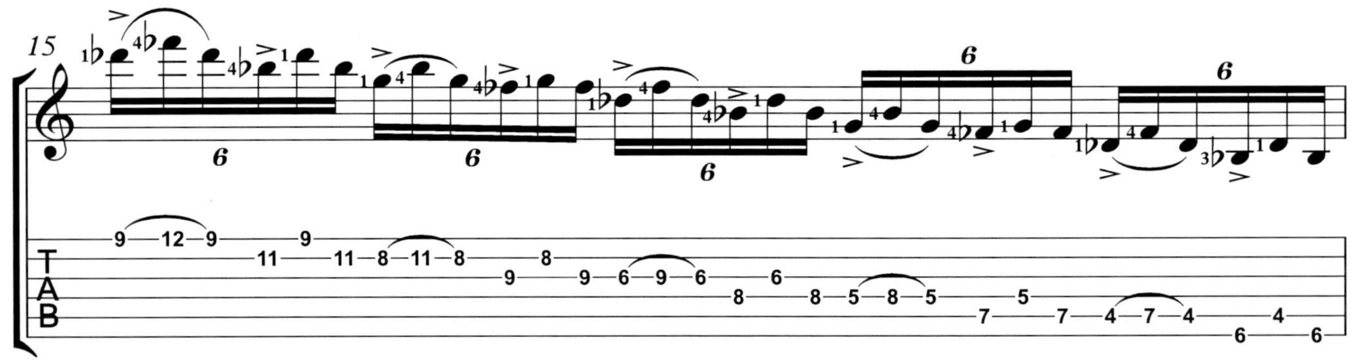
15
TAB

16
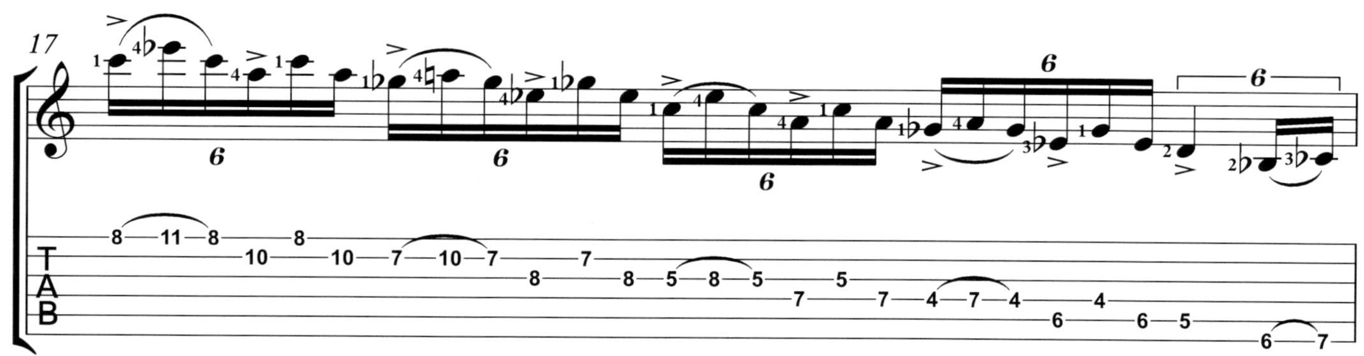
17
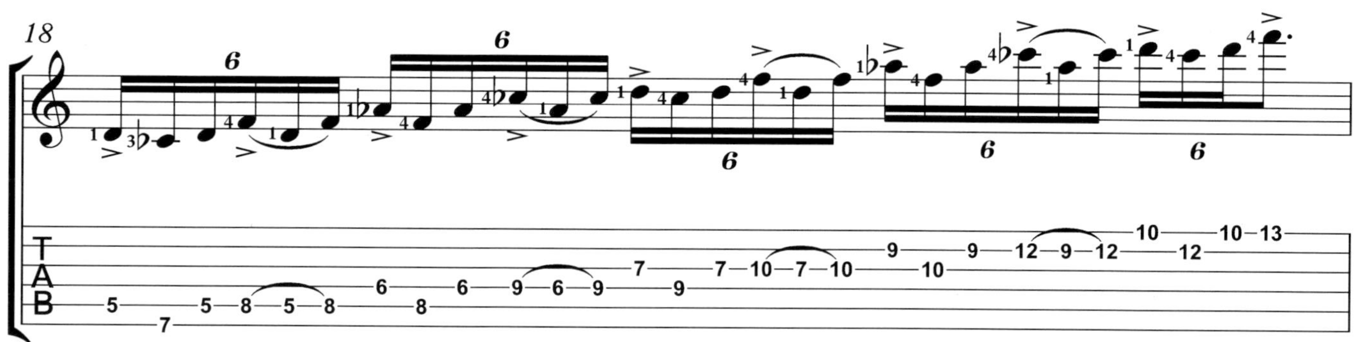
18
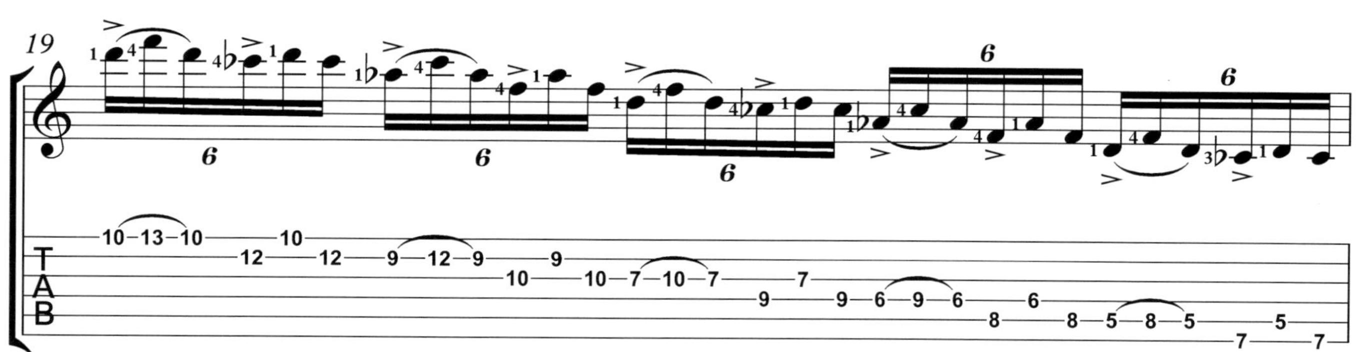
19

20

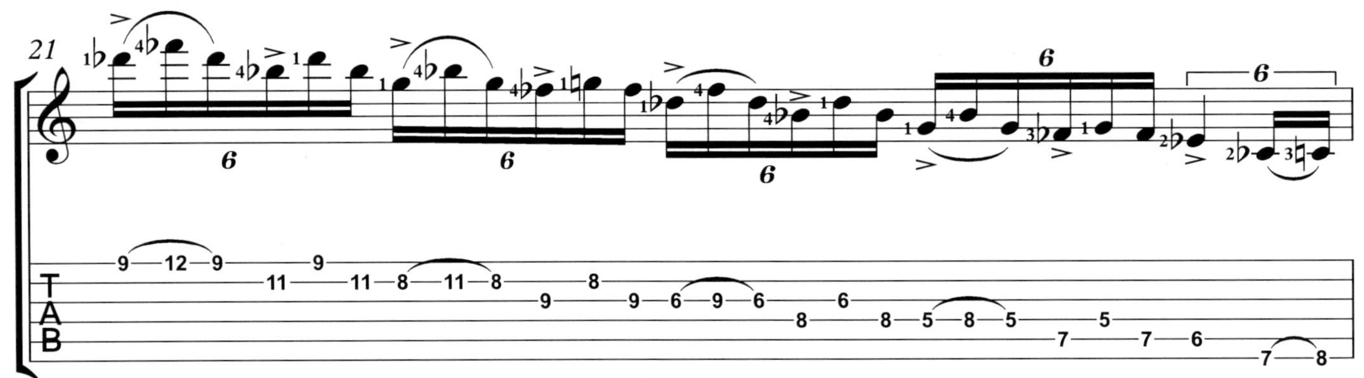

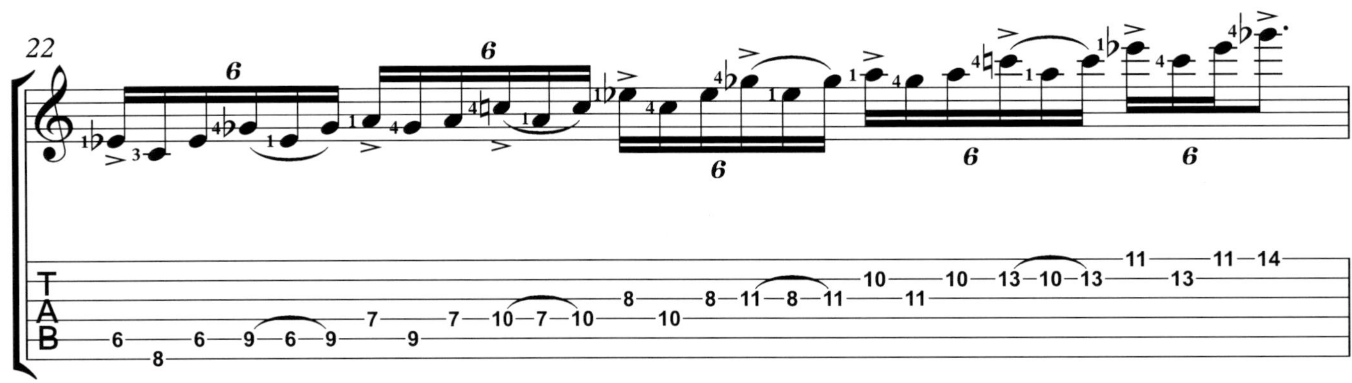

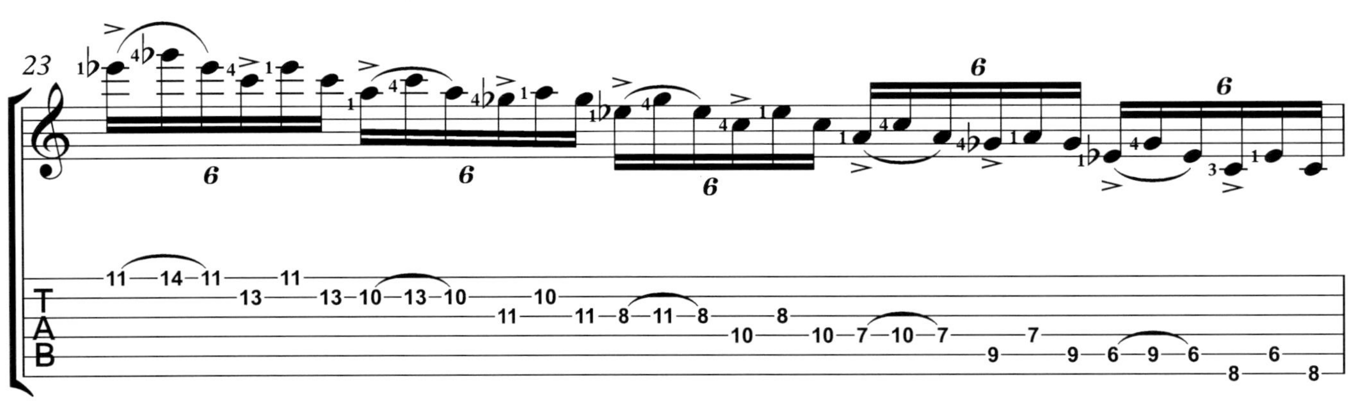

Speed Study

Music by YAGO SANTOS

Allegretto ♩=96

9
⑤
TAB
1—0—1—4—1—0—4—0—4—7—4—0—7—0—7—10—7—0—12—10—12—13—12—10—12

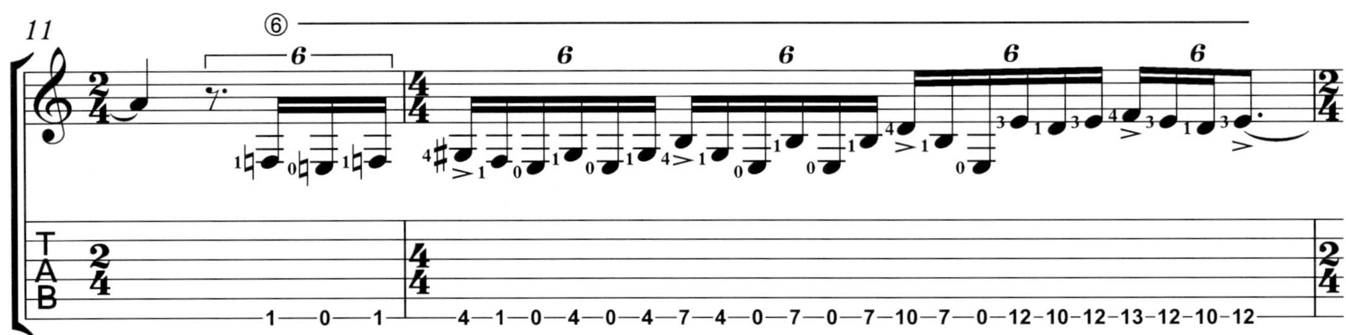
11
⑥
TAB
1—0—1—4—1—0—4—0—4—7—4—0—7—0—7—10—7—0—12—10—12—13—12—10—12

13
⑤
TAB
1—0—1—4—1—0—4—0—4—7—4—0—7—0—7—10—7—0—12—10—12—13—12—10—12

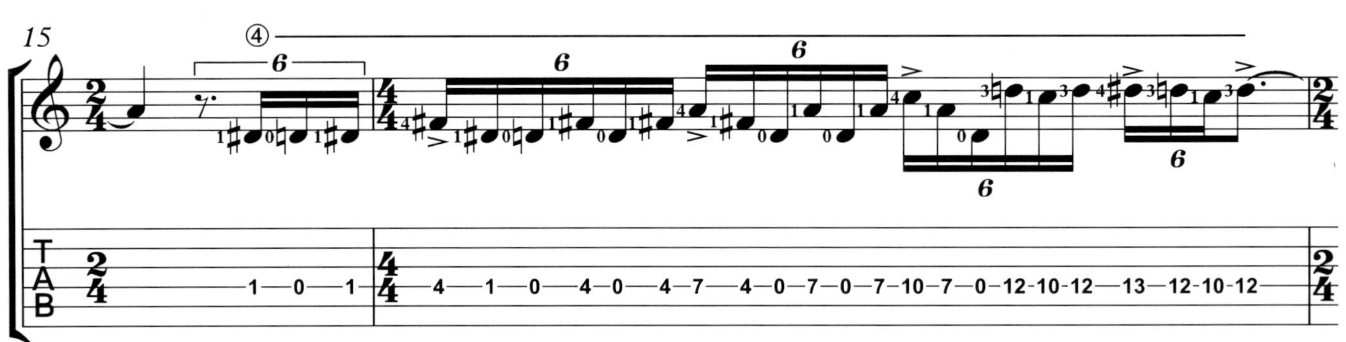
15
④
TAB
1—0—1—4—1—0—4—0—4—7—4—0—7—0—7—10—7—0—12—10—12—13—12—10—12

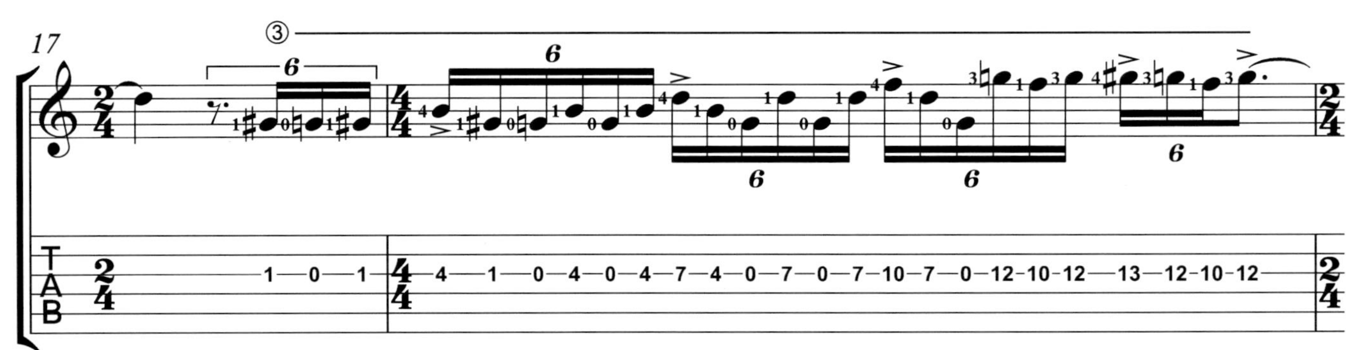
17
③
TAB
1—0—1—4—1—0—4—0—4—7—4—0—7—0—7—10—7—0—12—10—12—13—12—10—12

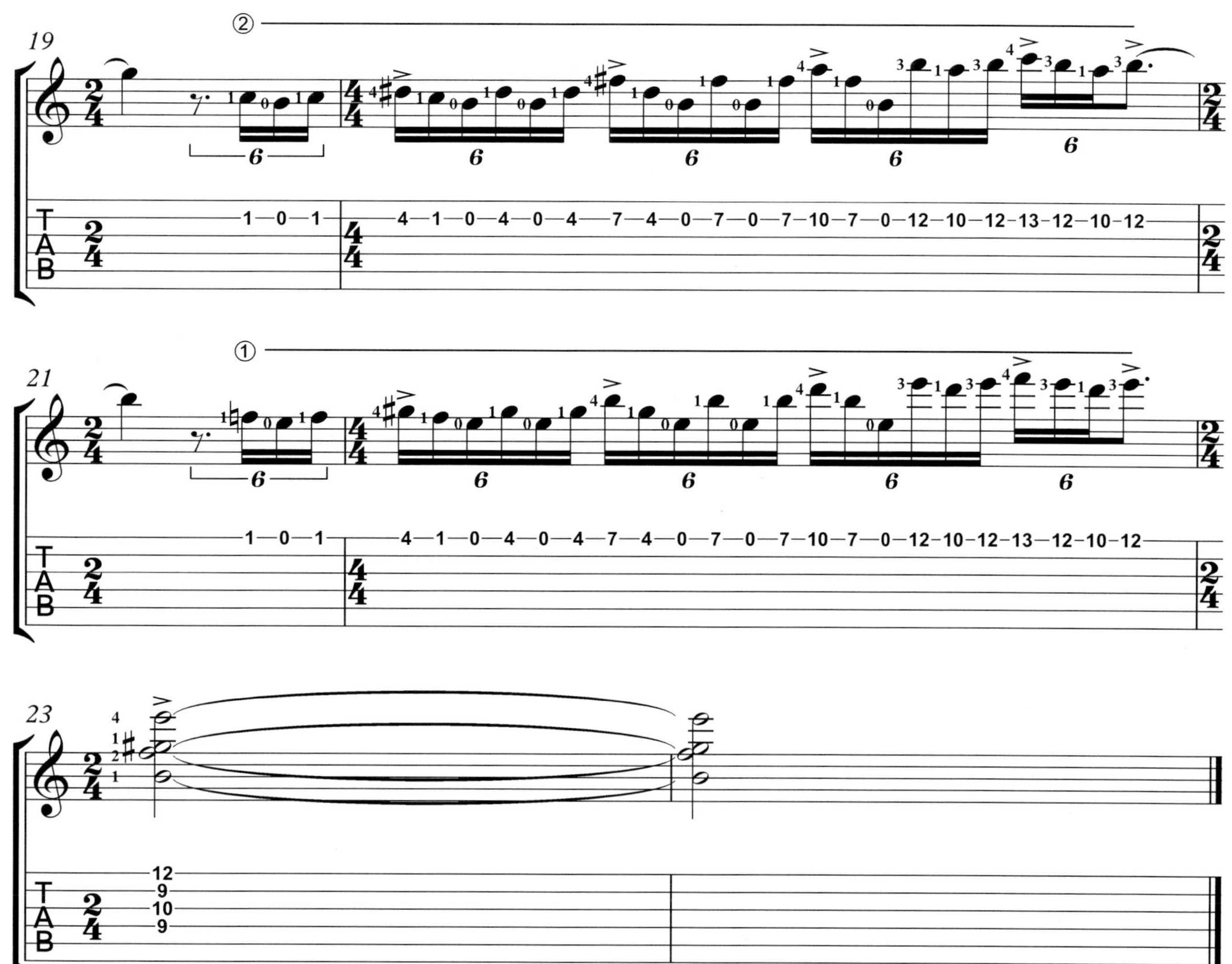
19
T
A
B
1—0—1
4—1—0—4—0—4—7—4—0—7—0—7—10—7—0—12—10—12—13—12—10—12
21
1—0—1
4—1—0—4—0—4—7—4—0—7—0—7—10—7—0—12—10—12—13—12—10—12
23
12
9
10
9

Arpegio Study I

Allegro ♩=155

Music by YAGO SANTOS

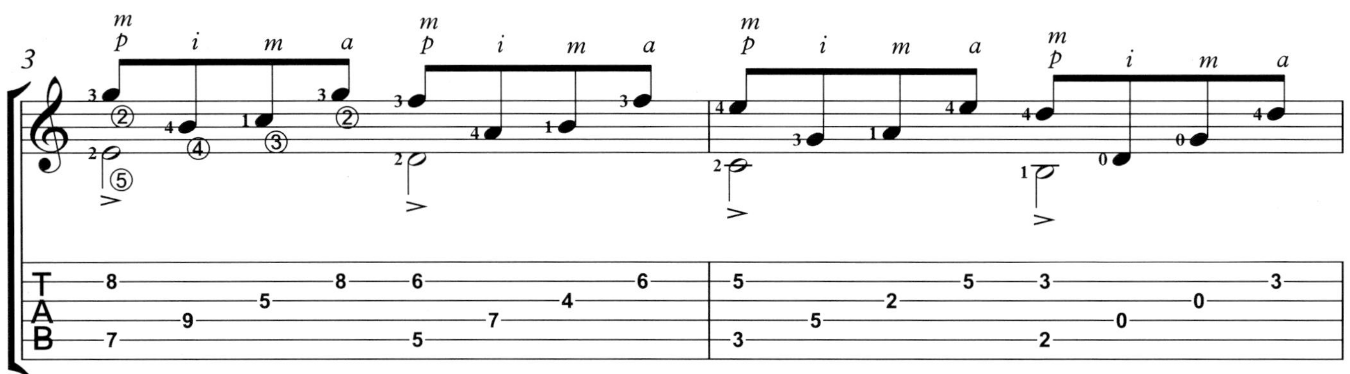

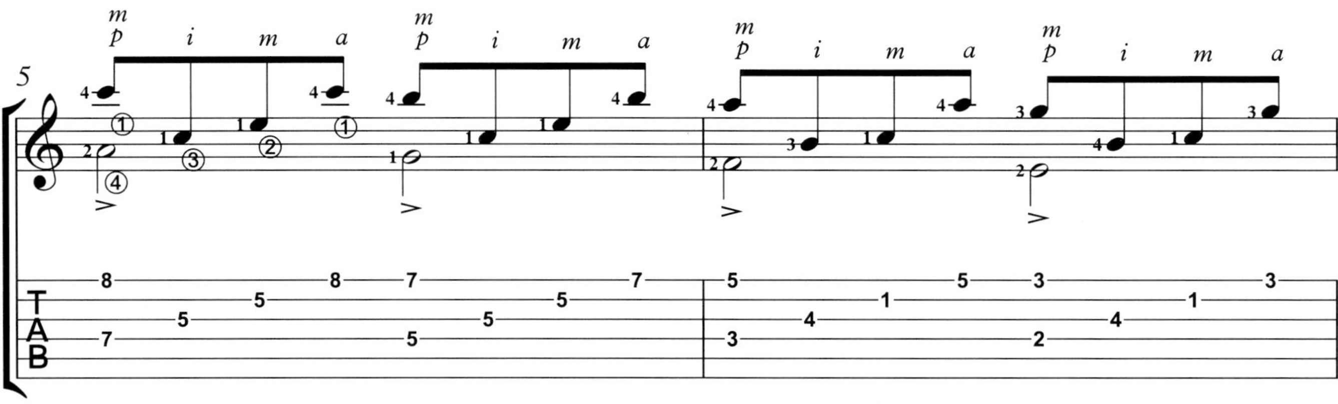

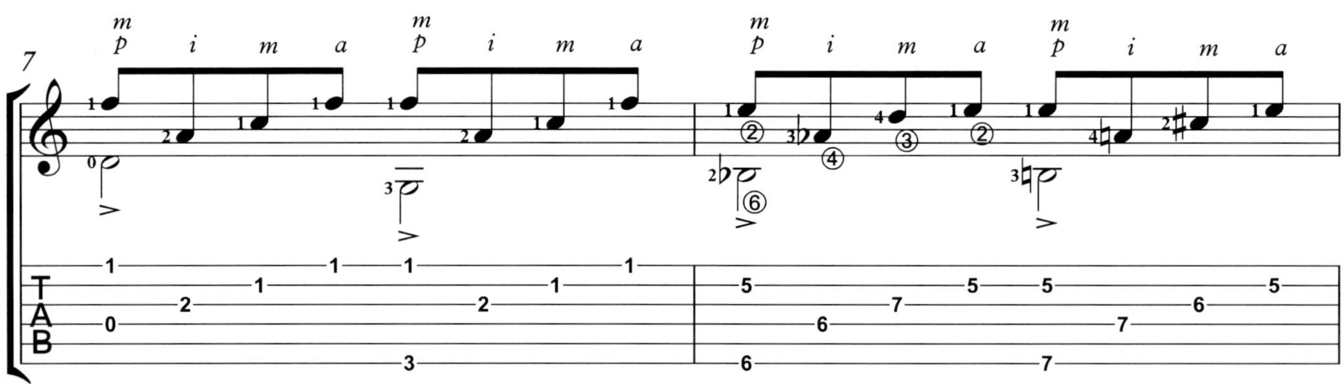

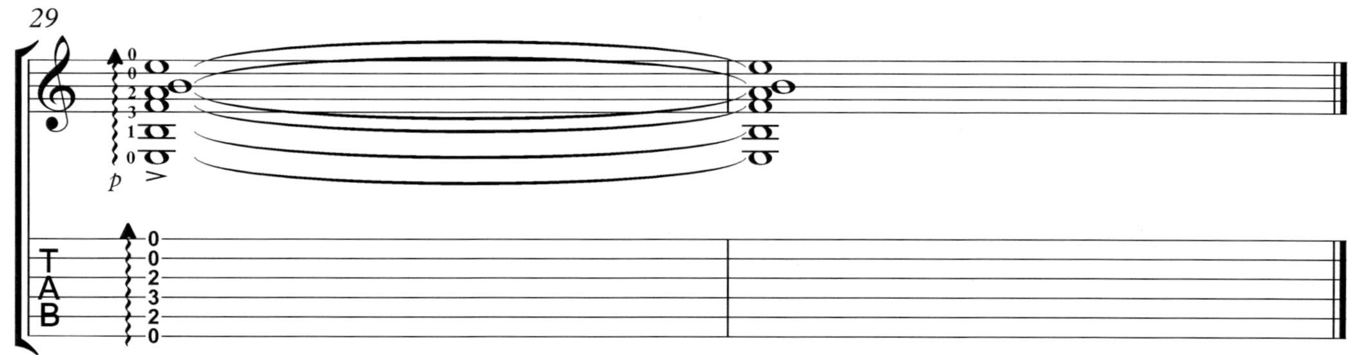
29
p
T
A
B
0
0
2
3
2
0

Double Arpegio Study

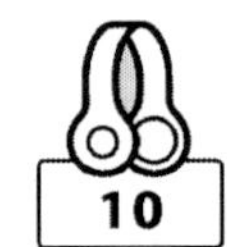

Music by YAGO SANTOS

Vivace ♩=125

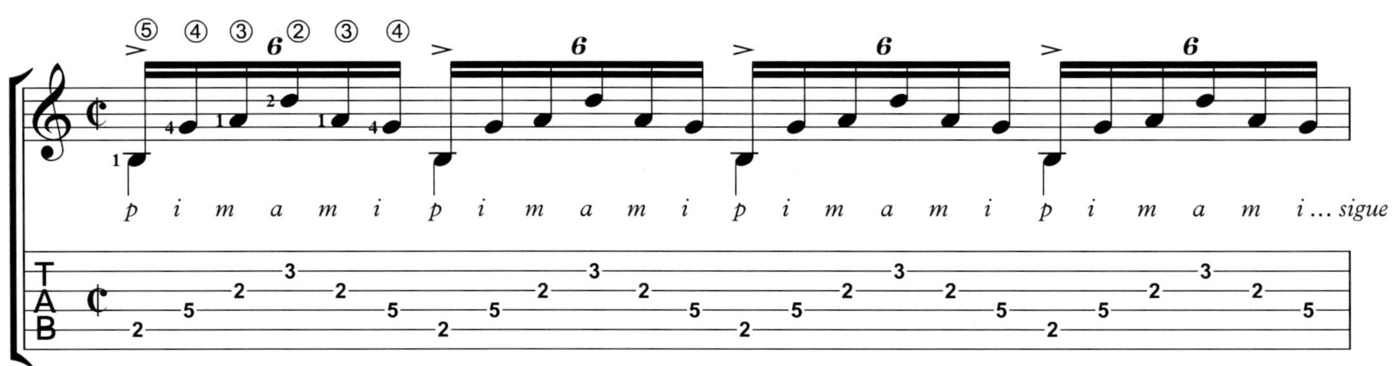

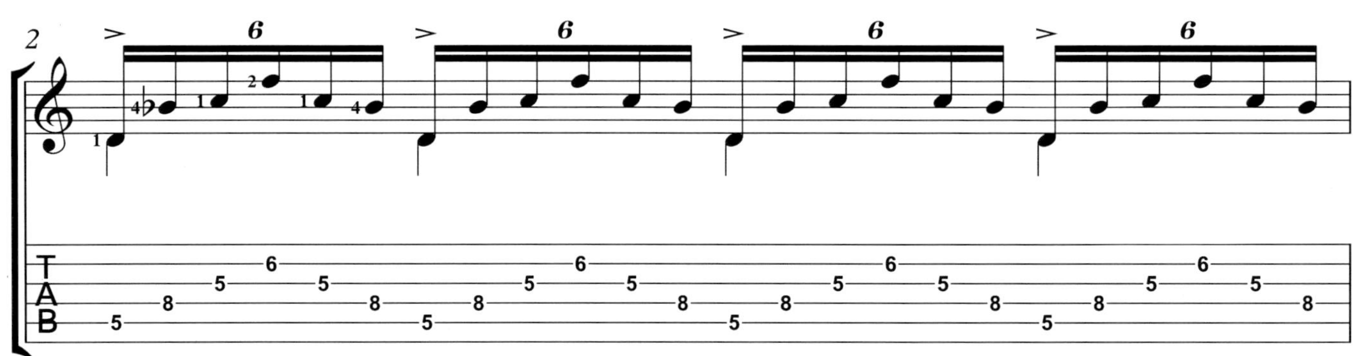

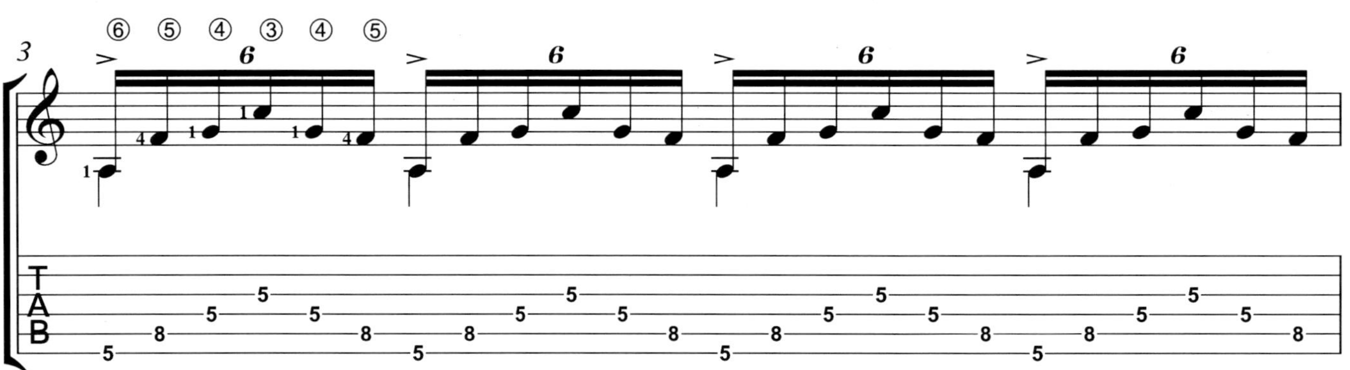

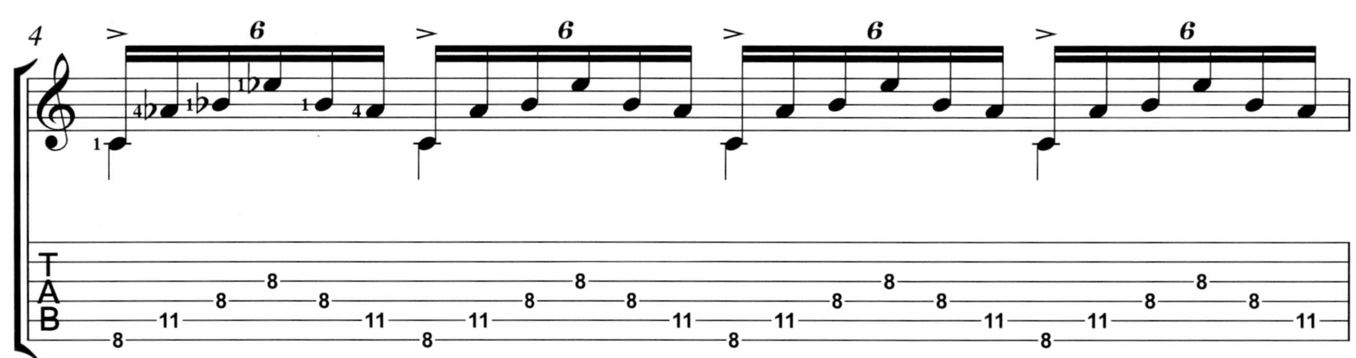

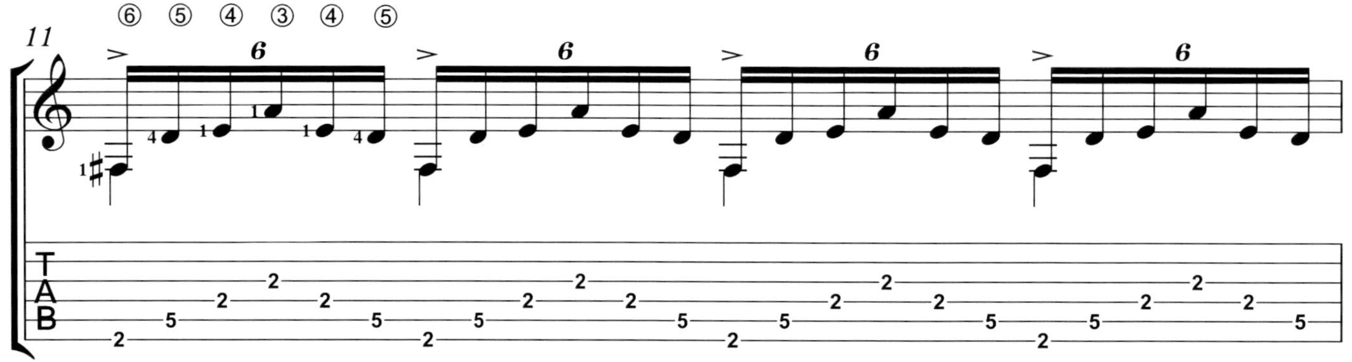
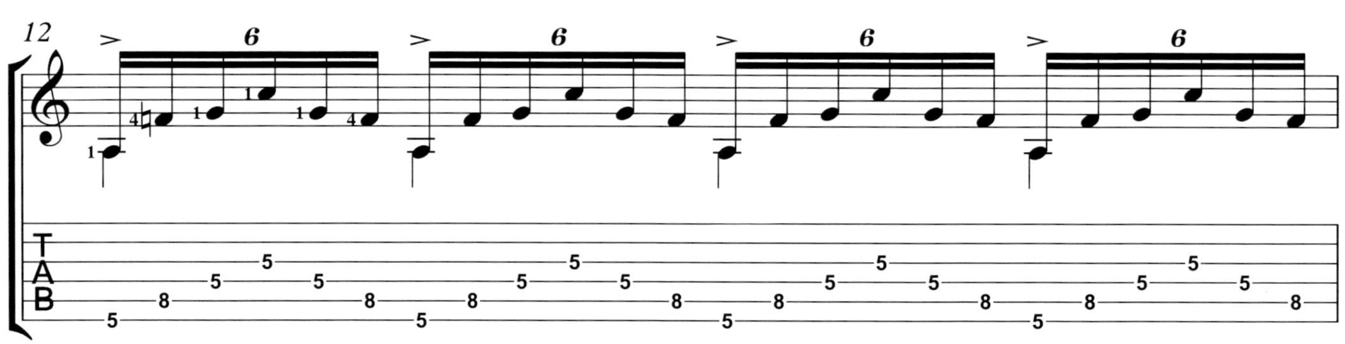
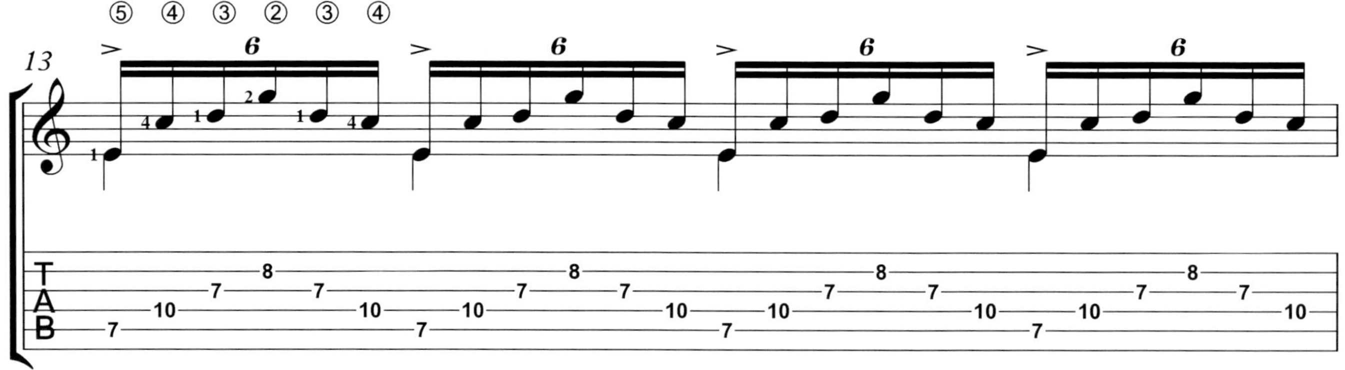
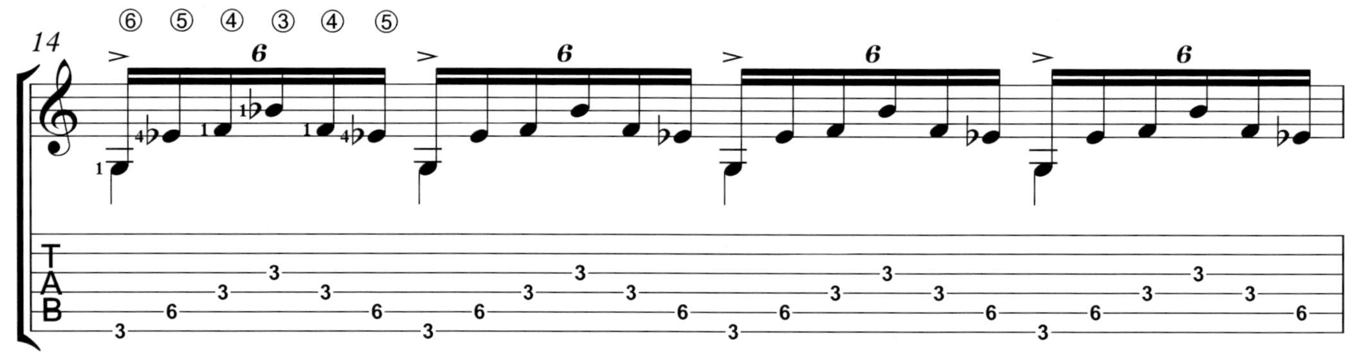

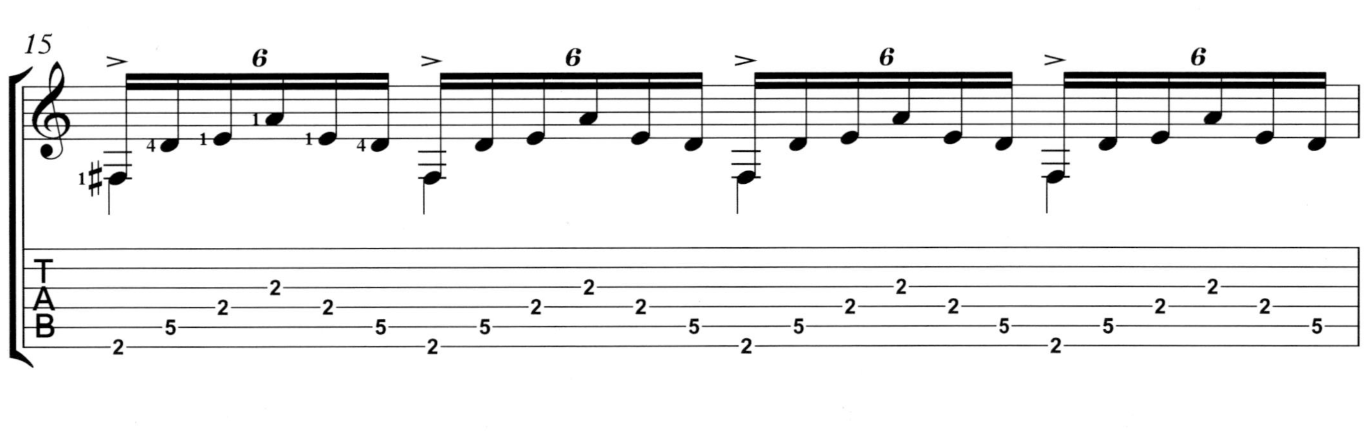
15
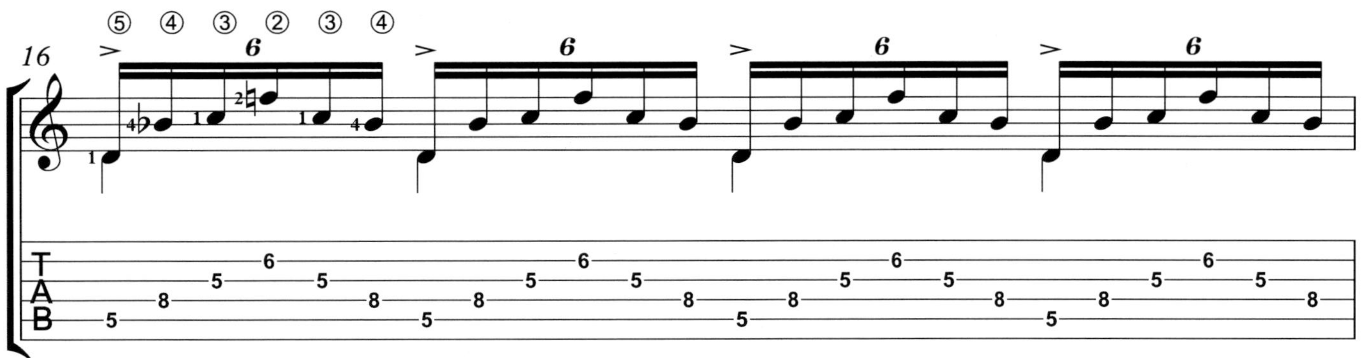
16
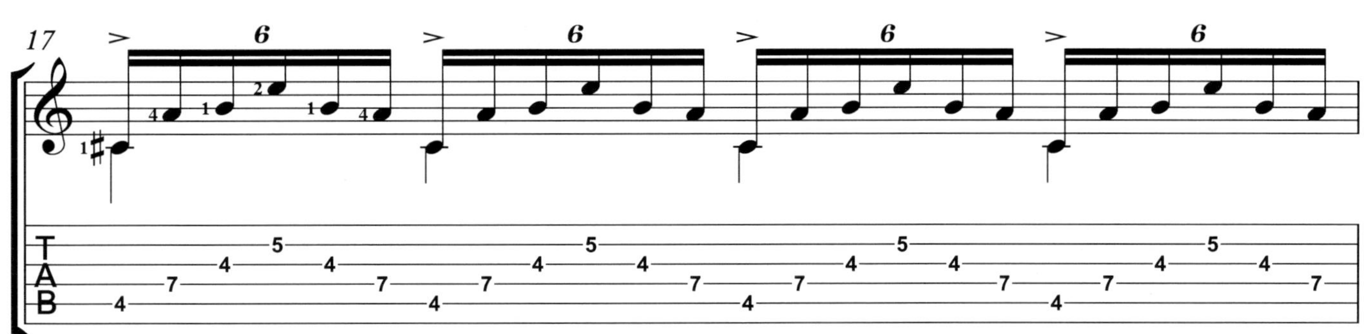
17
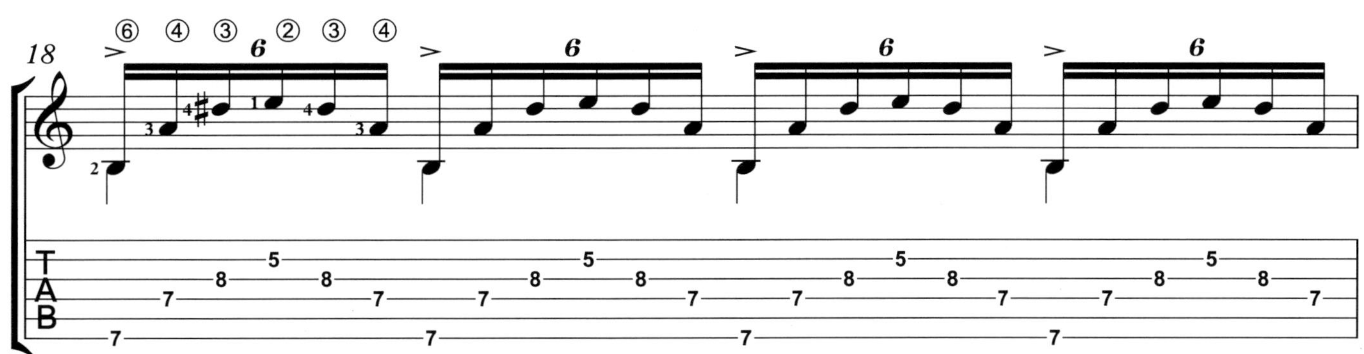
18
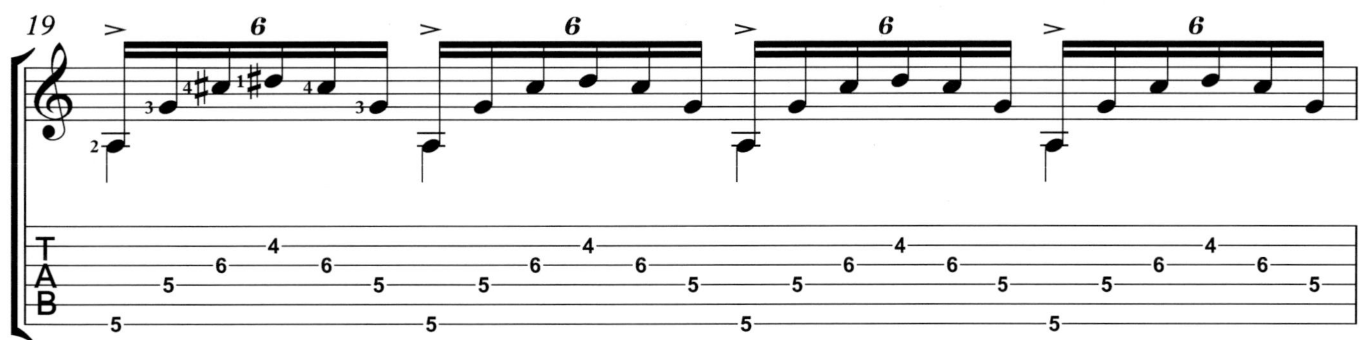
19

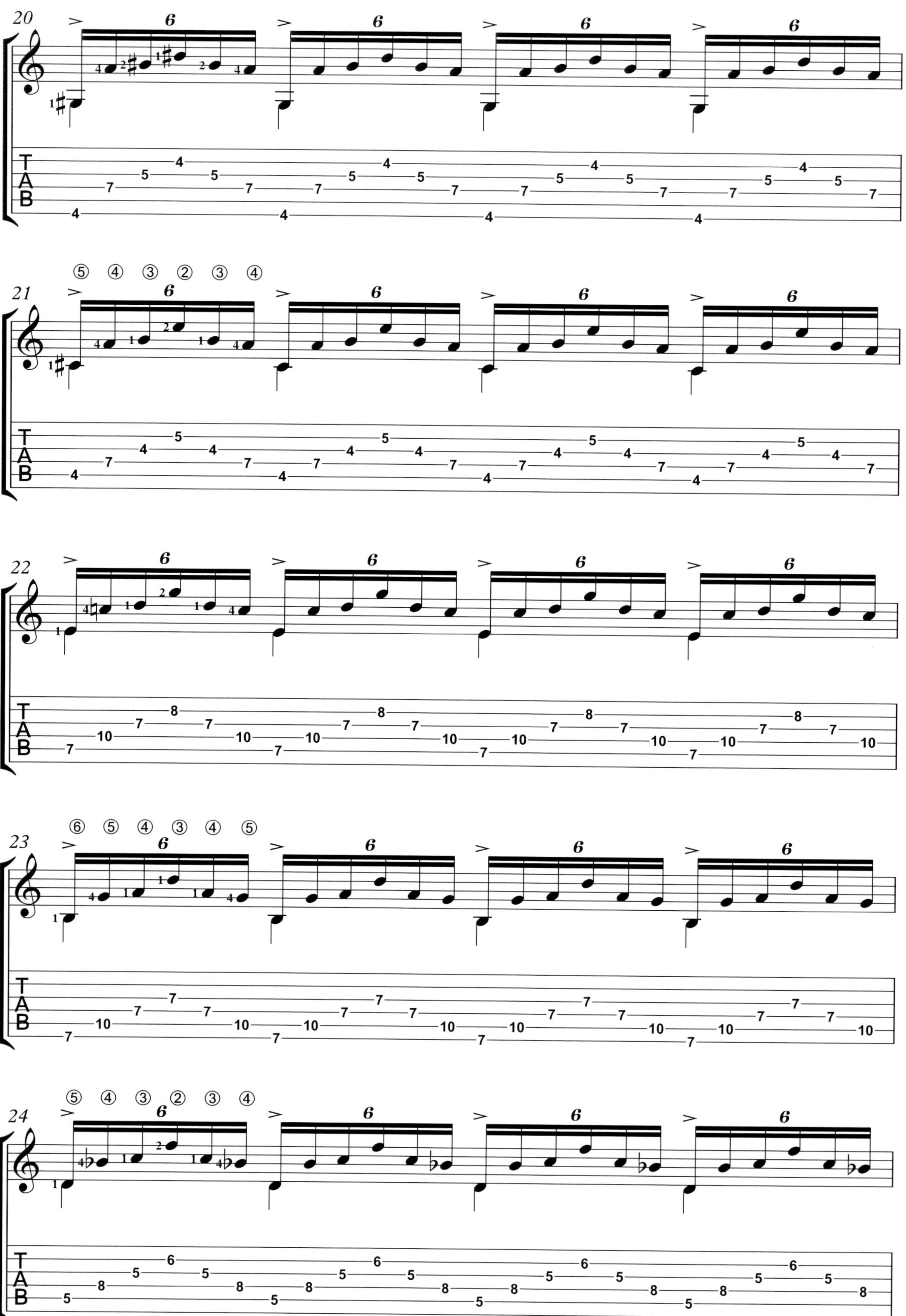
20
6
T
A
B
21
⑤ ④ ③ ② ③ ④
22
23
⑥ ⑤ ④ ③ ④ ⑤
24
⑤ ④ ③ ② ③ ④

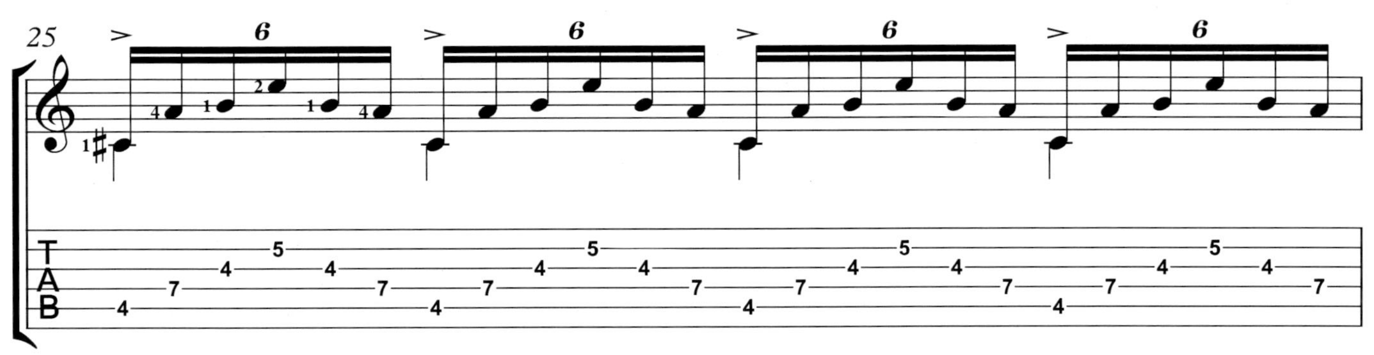
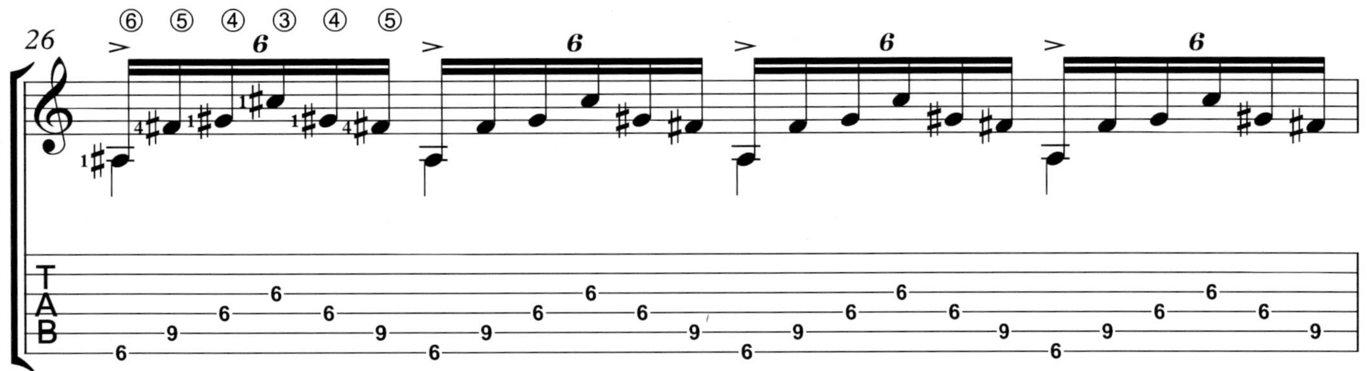
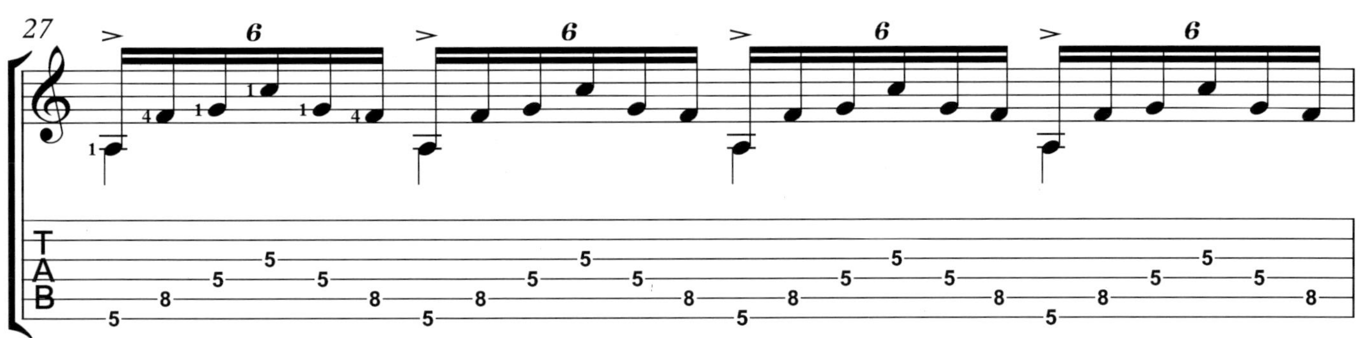
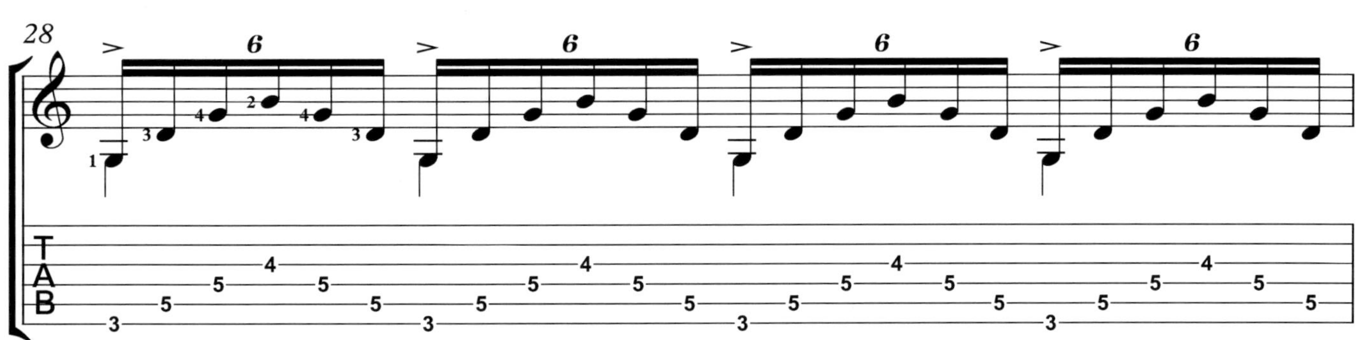
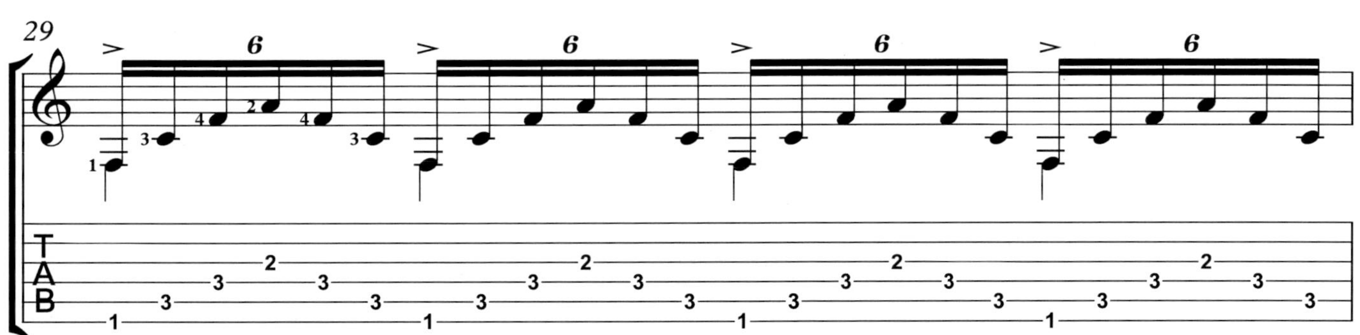

30
6 6 6 6
T
A
B

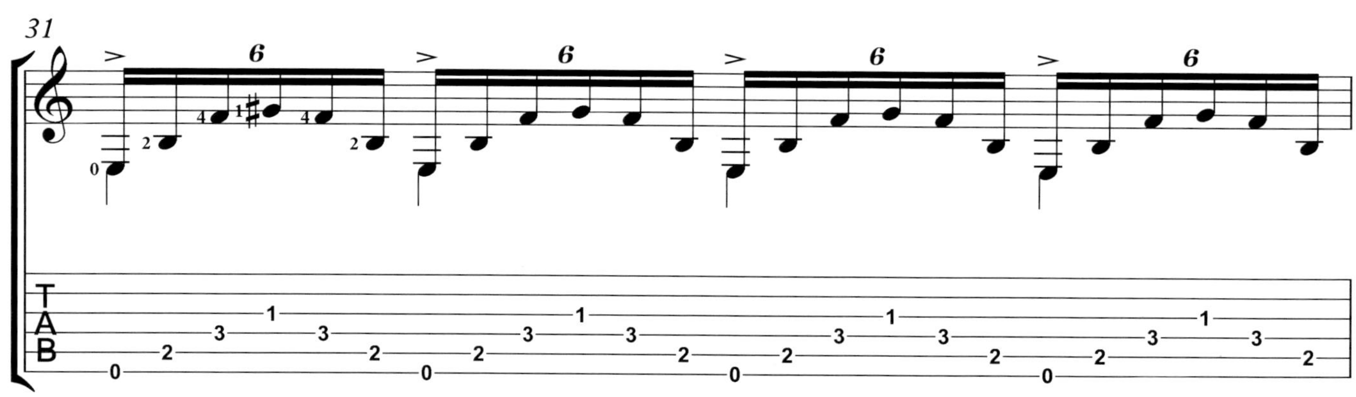
31
6 6 6 6
T
A
B

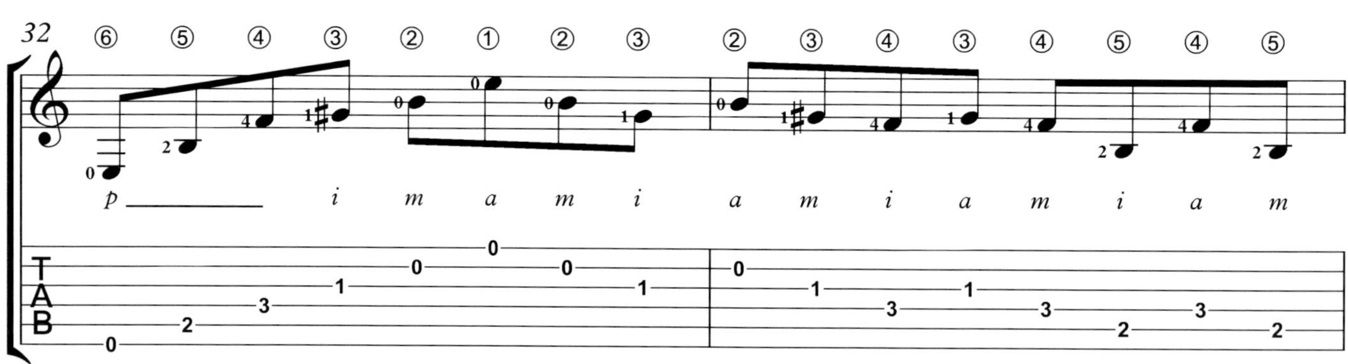
32
⑥ ⑤ ④ ③ ② ① ② ③ ② ③ ④ ③ ④ ⑤ ④ ⑤
p i m a m i a m i a m i a m
T
A
B

34
p
T
A
B

This page has been left blank to avoid an awkward page turn.

Pulgar-Indice Study

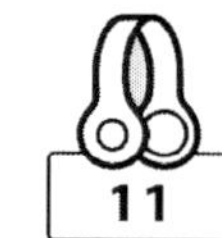

Allegro ♩.=*115*

Music by YAGO SANTOS

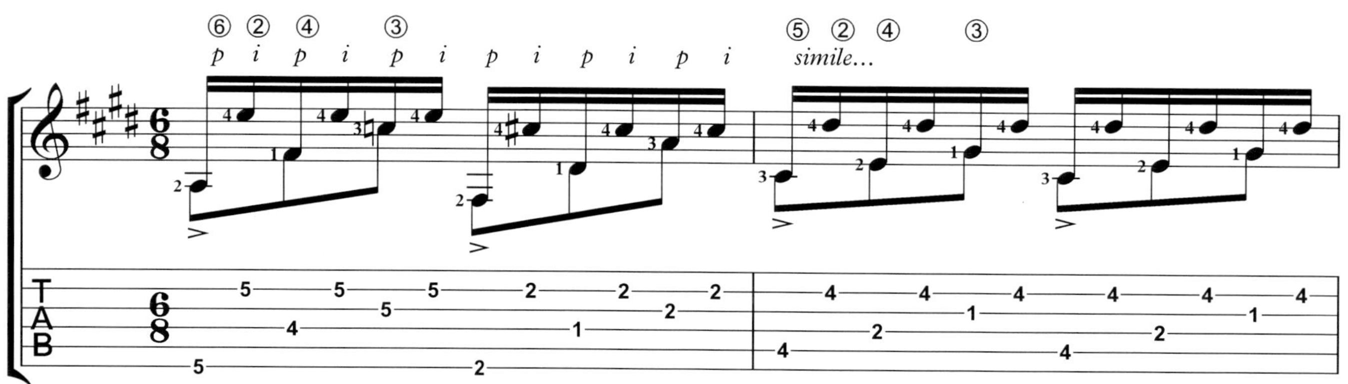

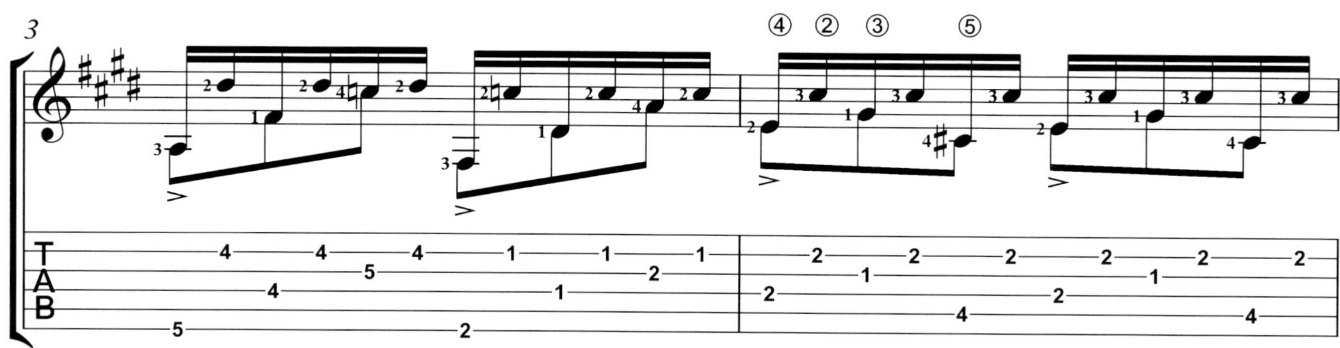

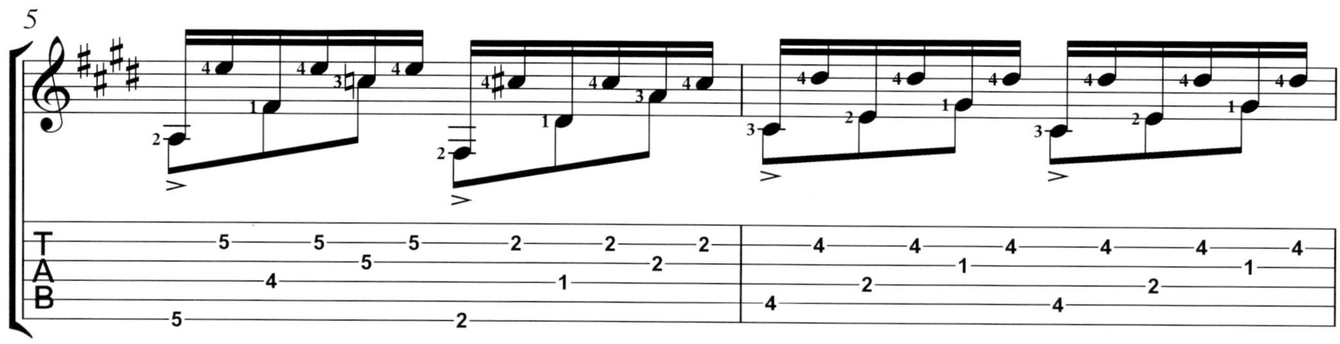

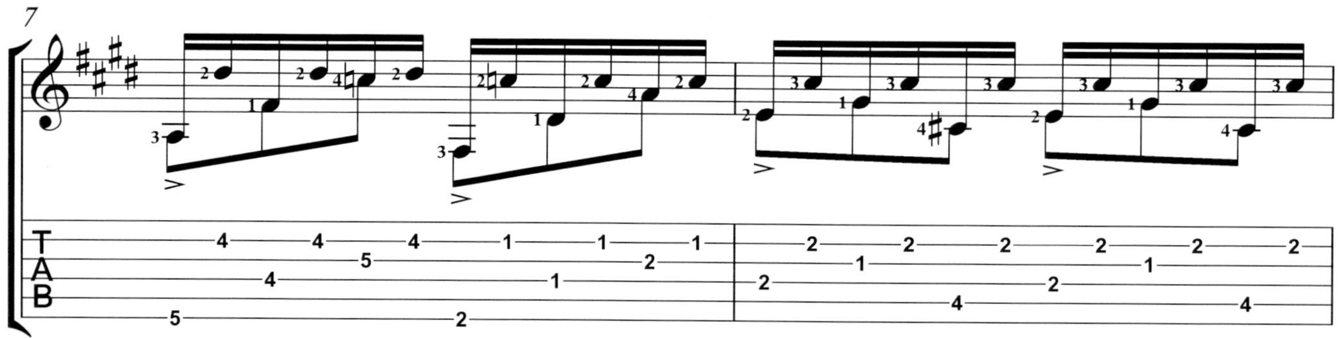

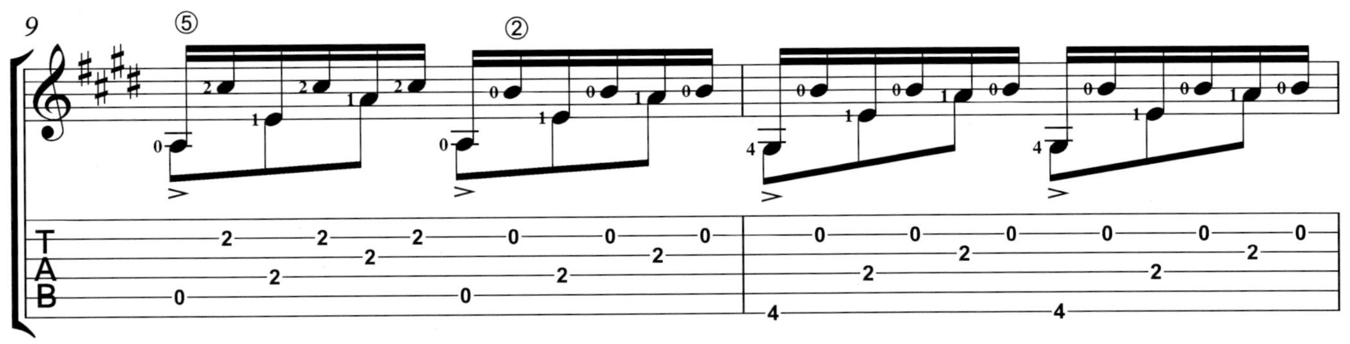

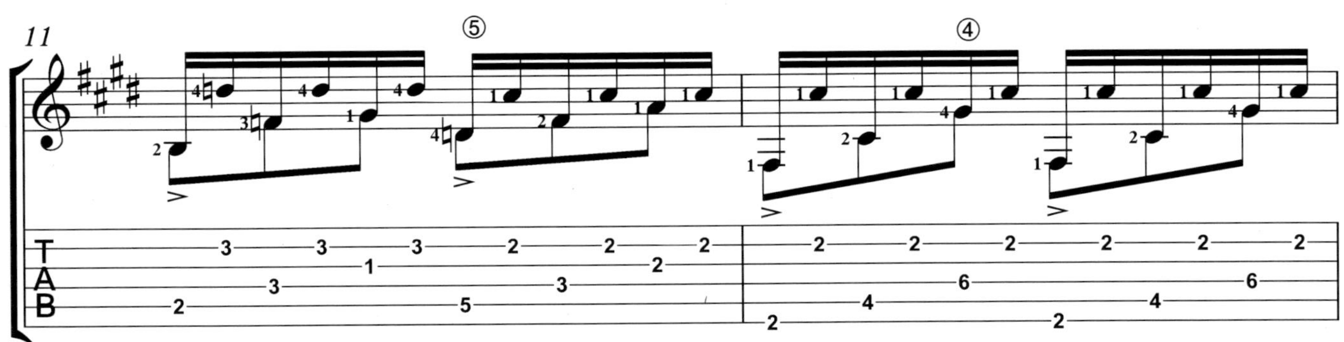

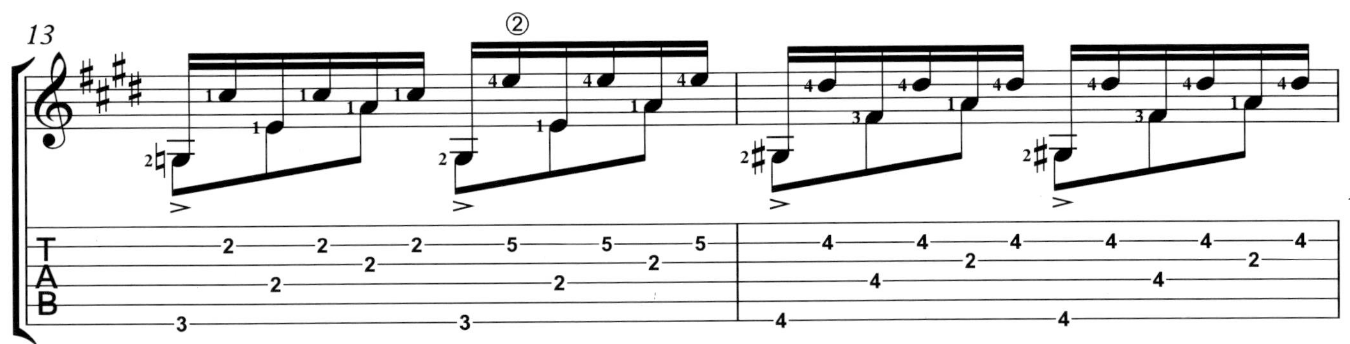

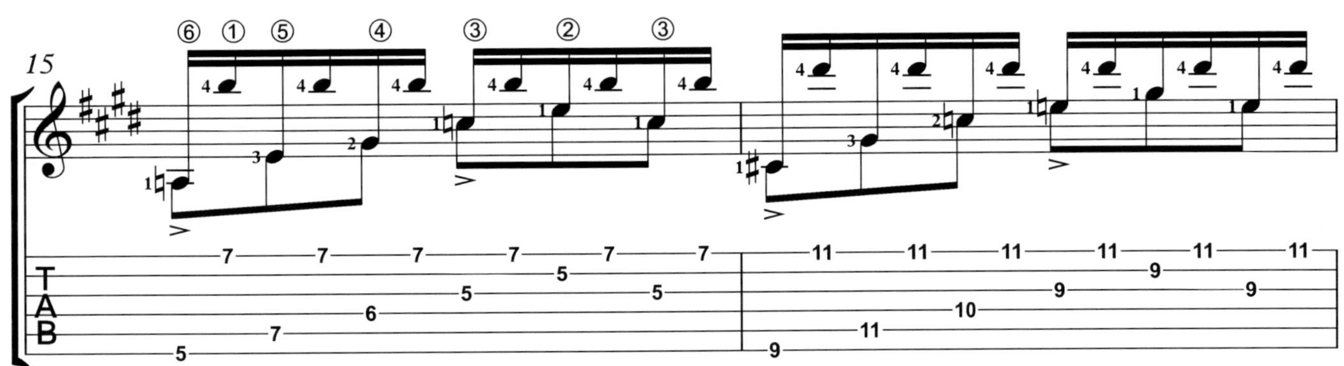

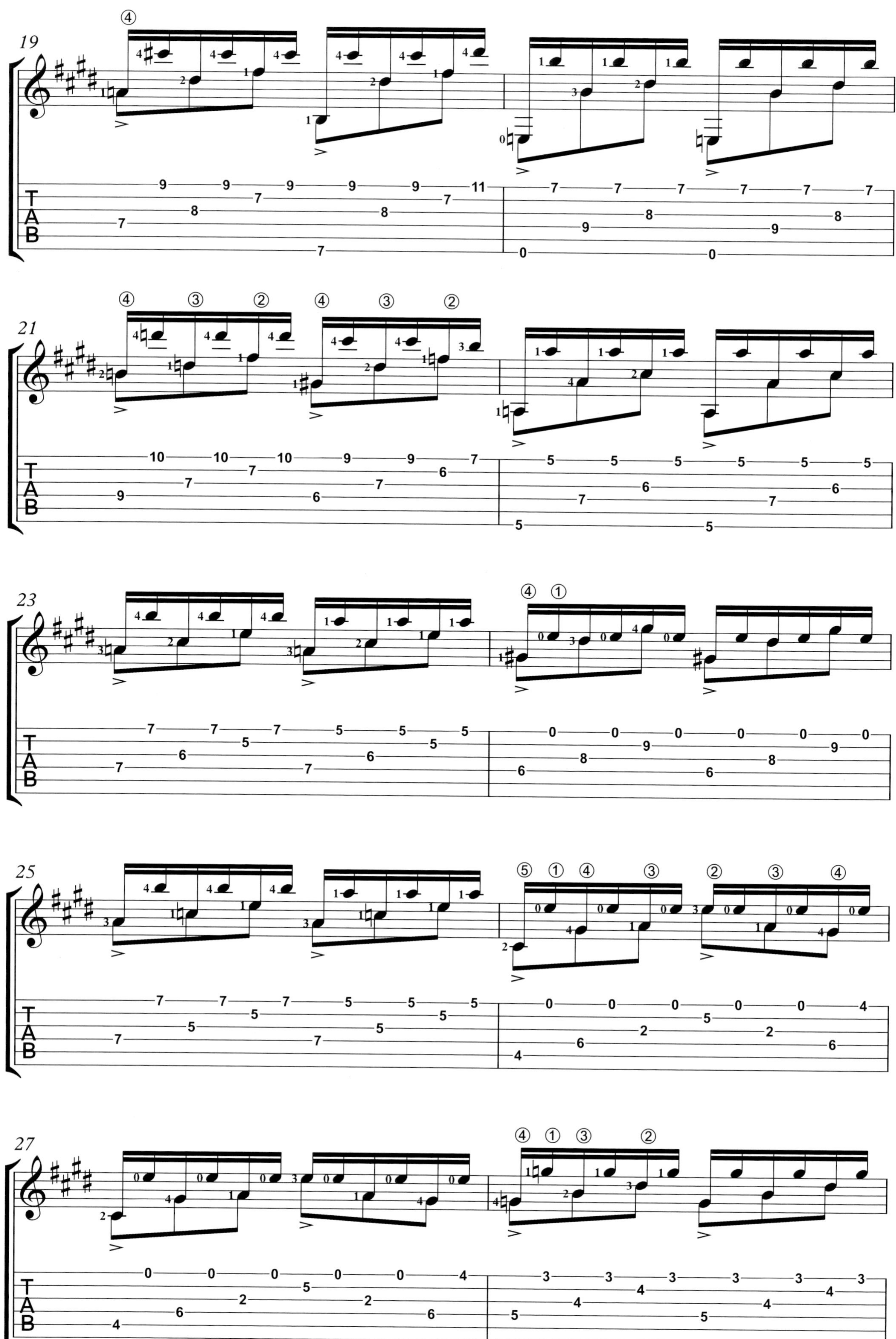
19
TAB
21
TAB
23
TAB
25
TAB
27
TAB

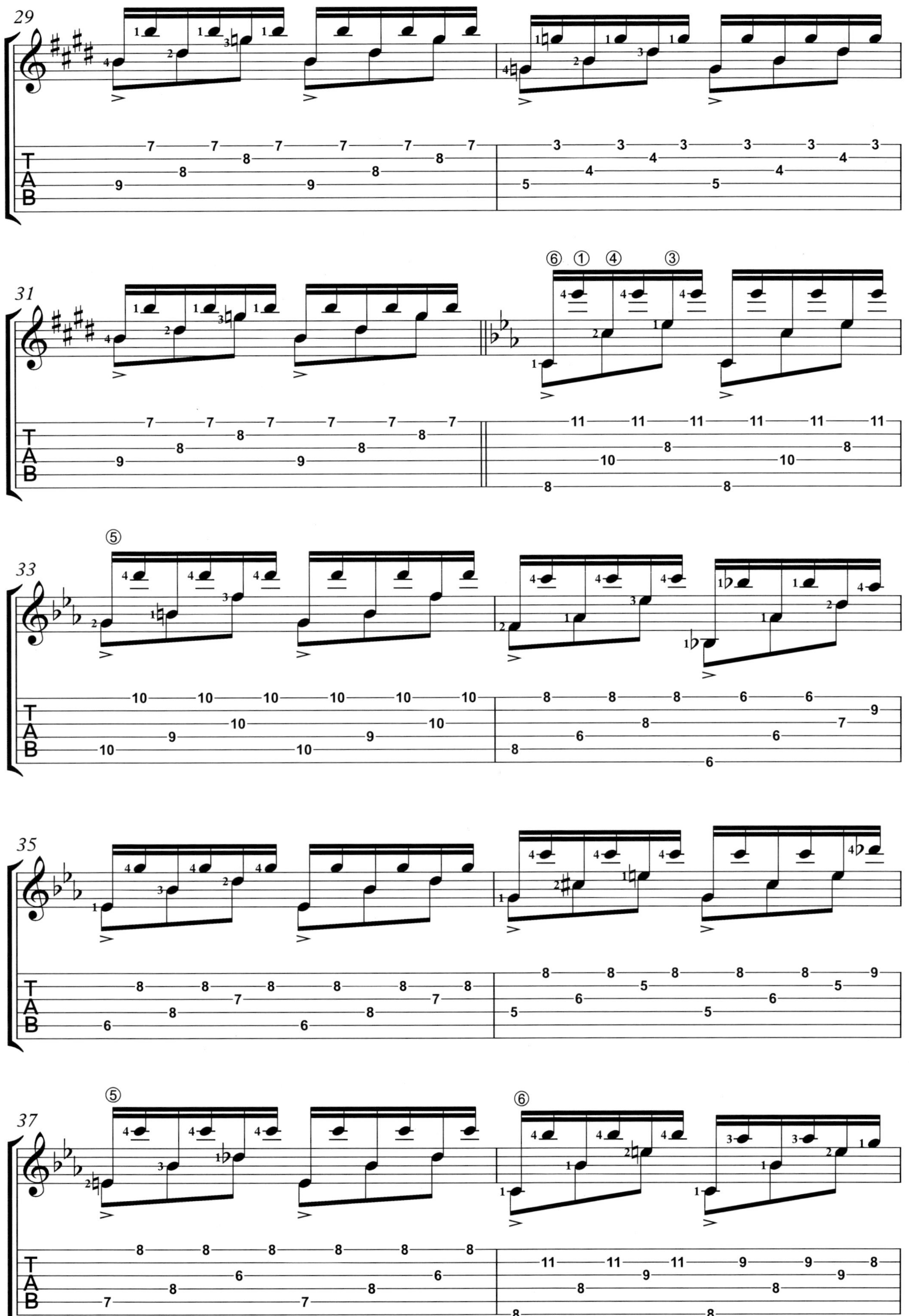

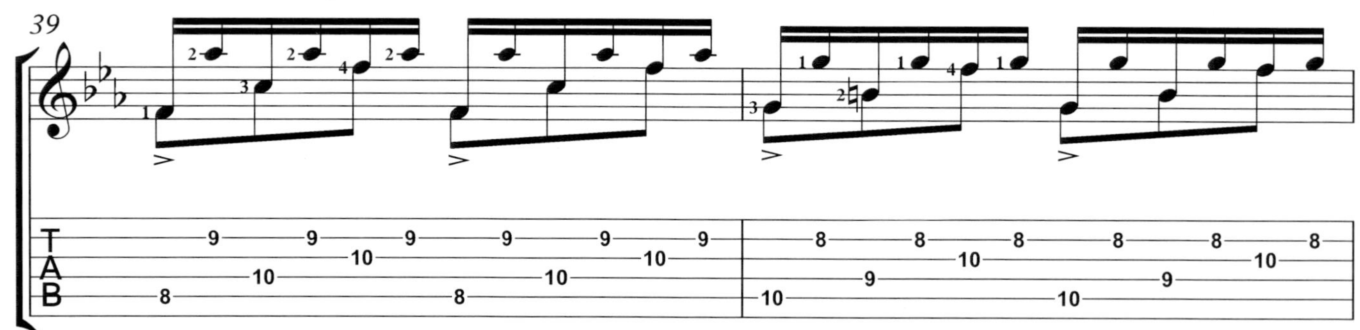
39
TAB
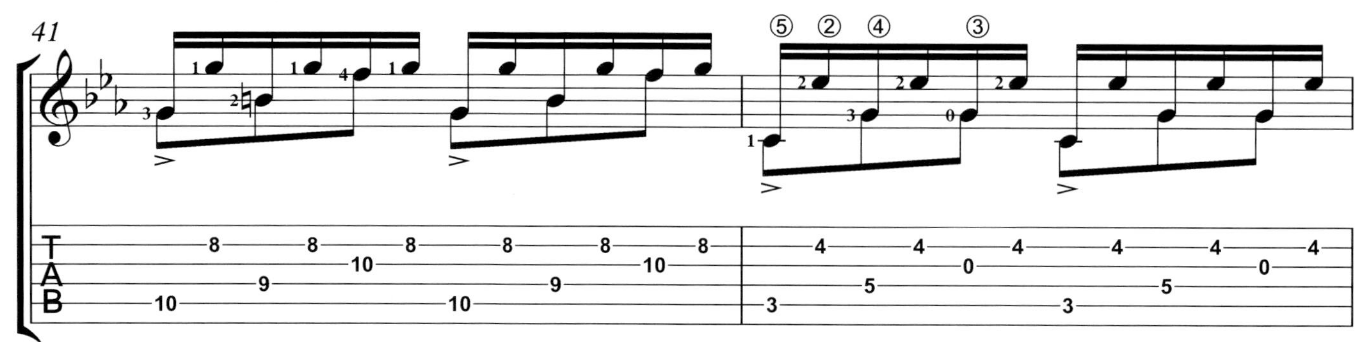
41
TAB
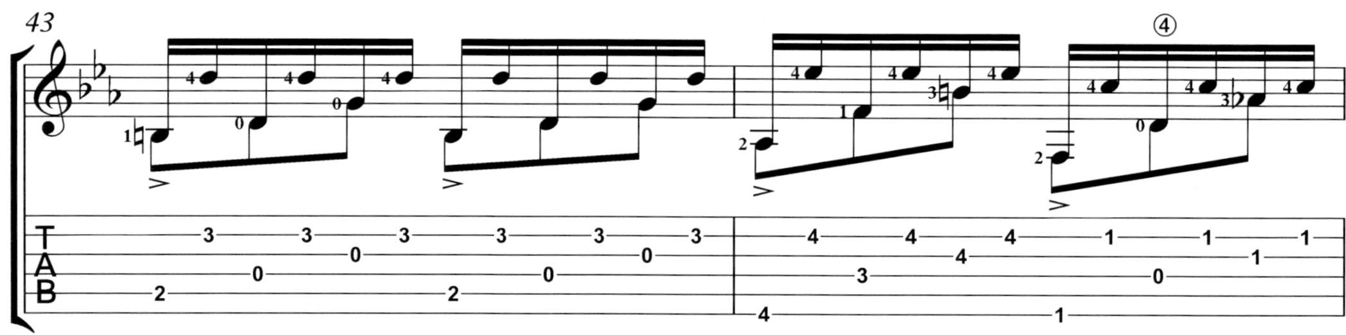
43
TAB
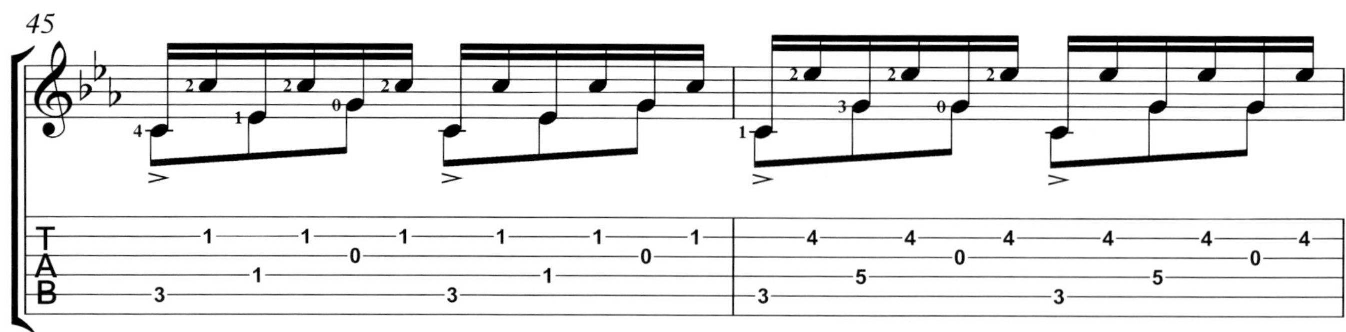
45
TAB
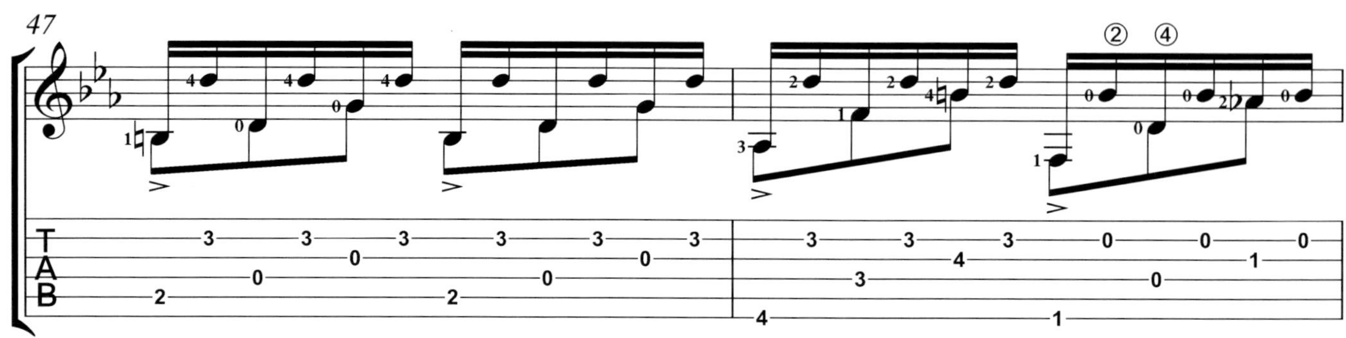
47
TAB

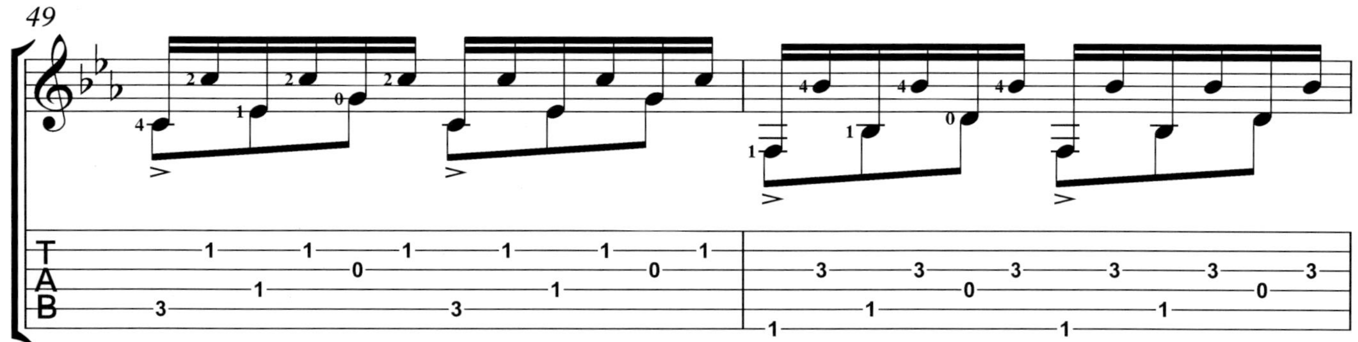

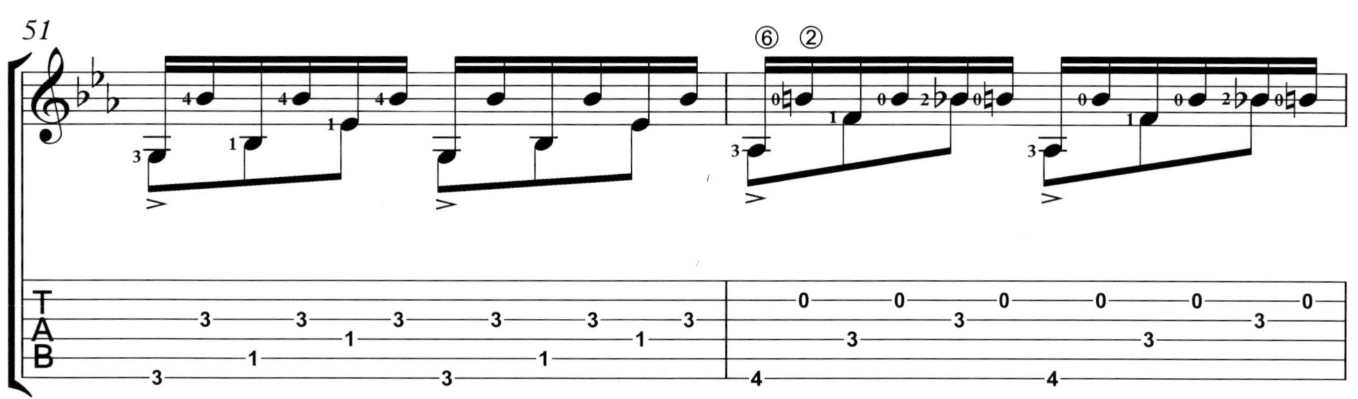

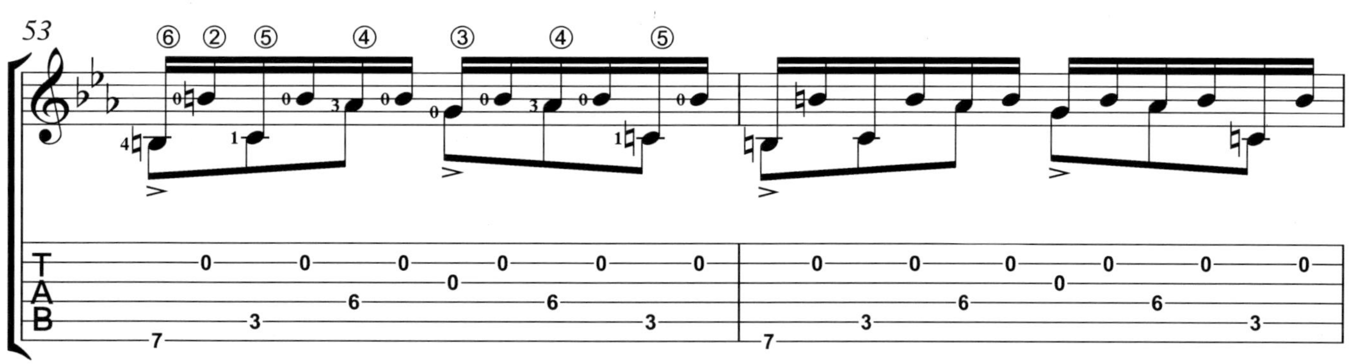

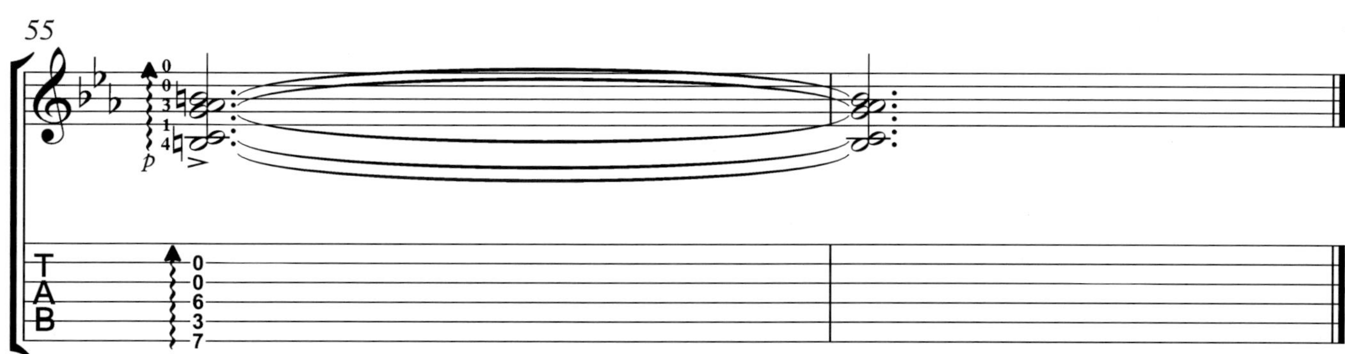

Tremolo Study I

Vivace ♩=140

Music by YAGO SANTOS

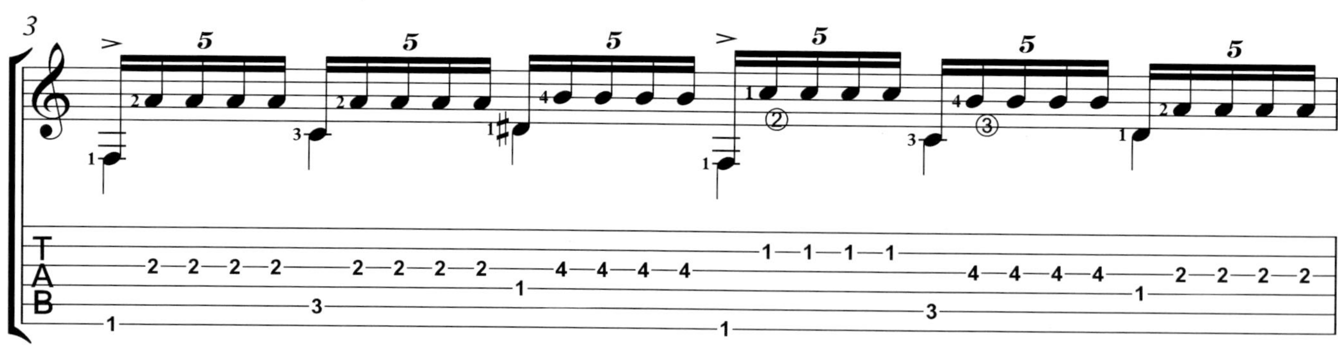

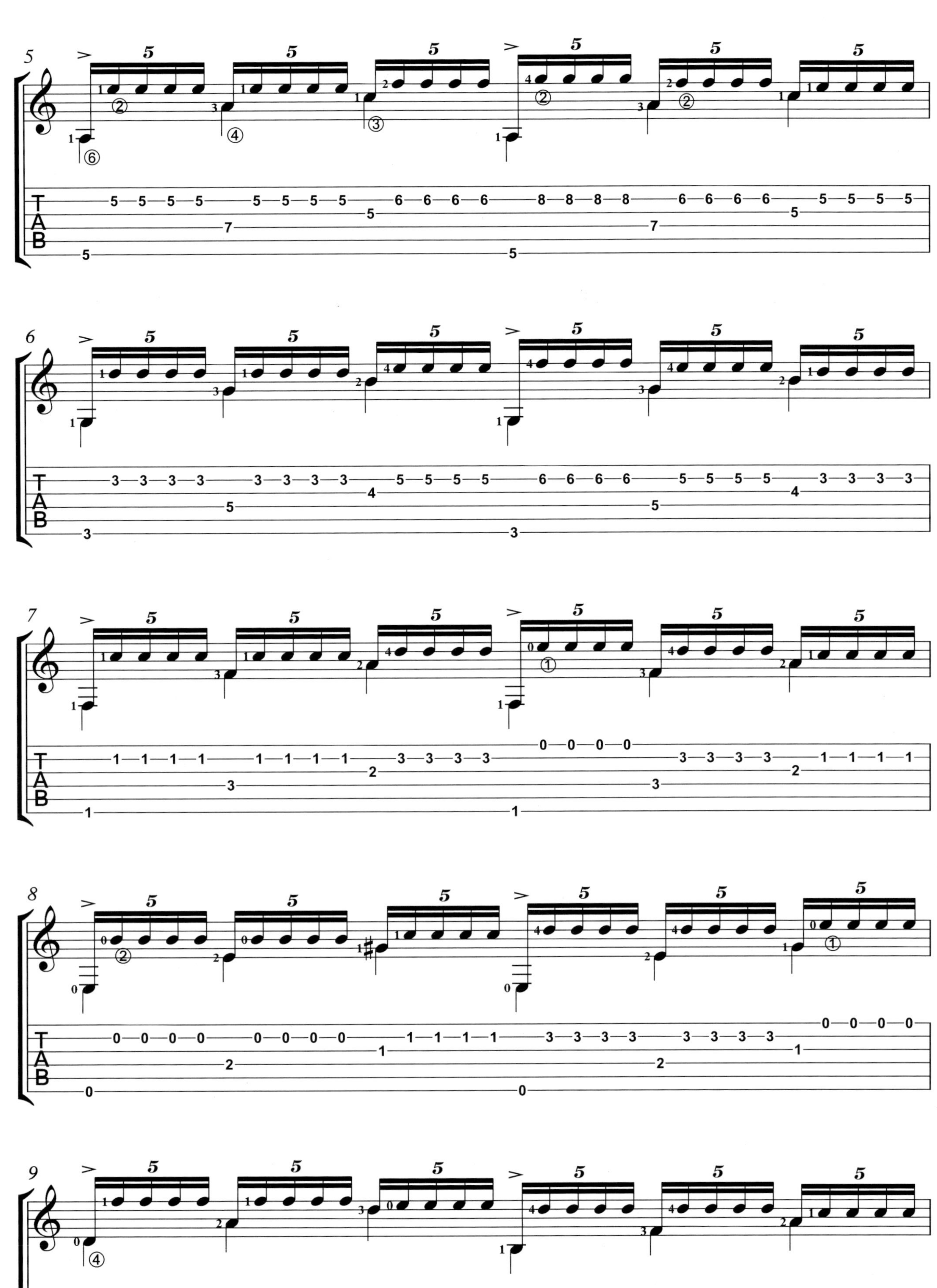

12

13

14

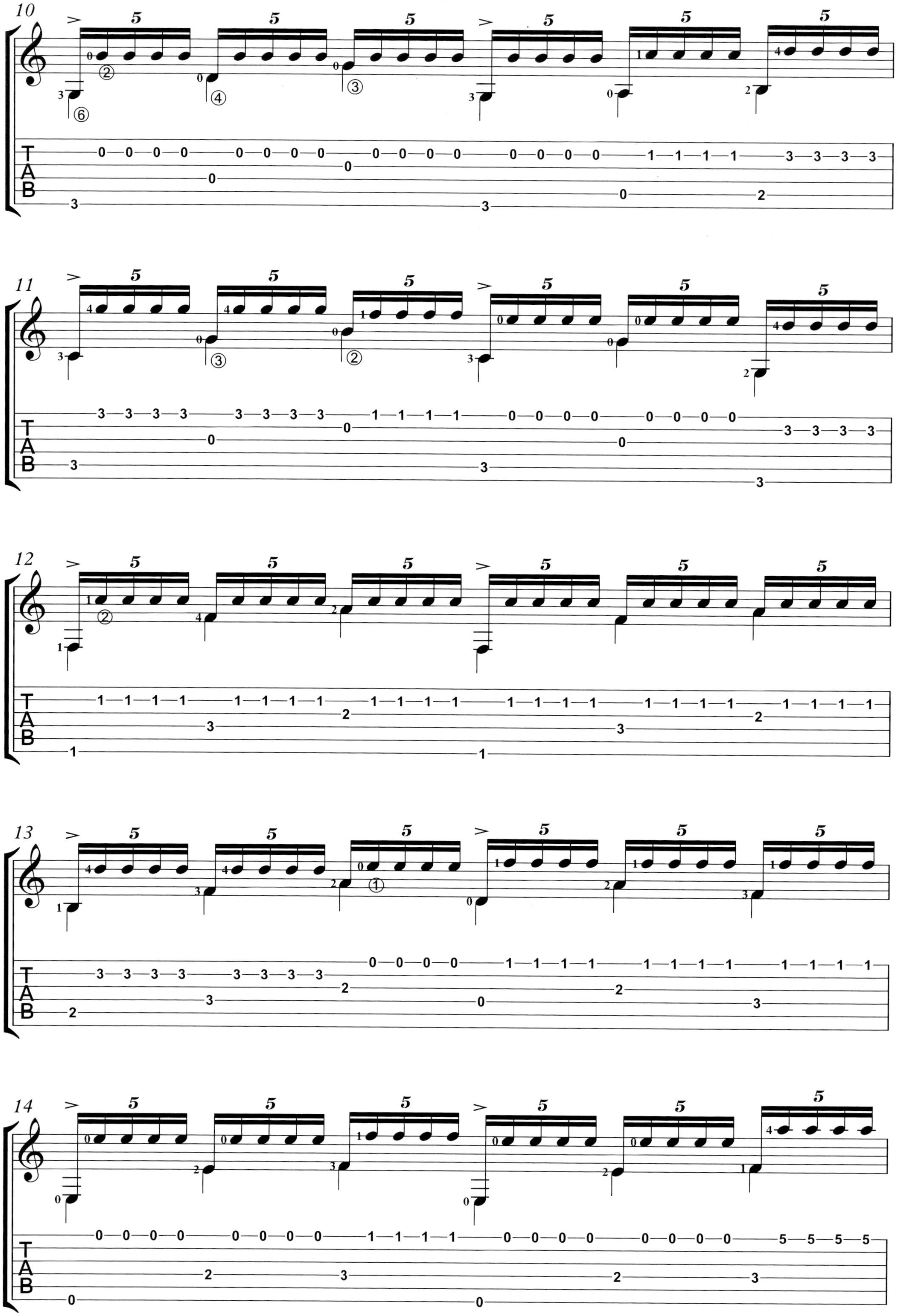

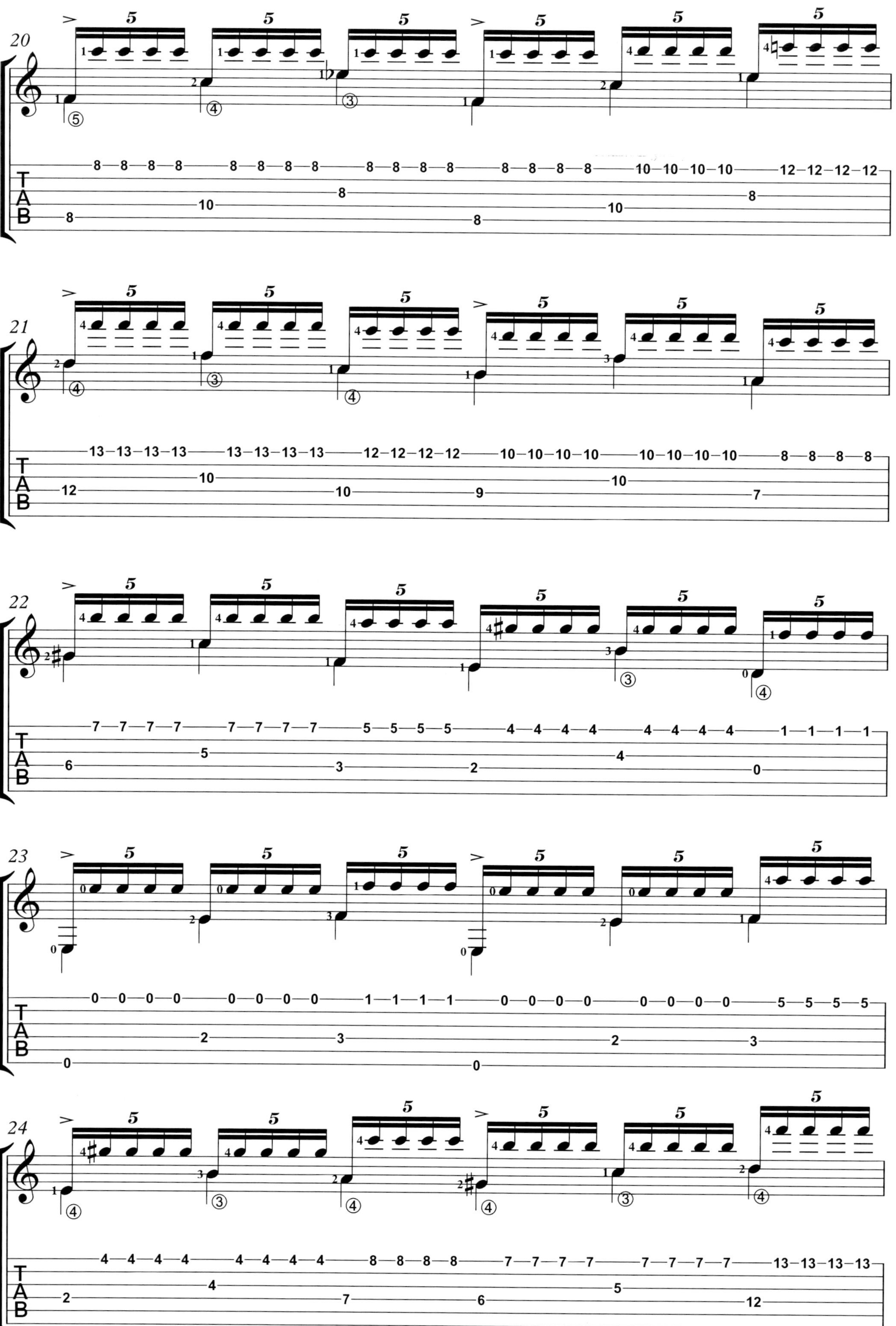

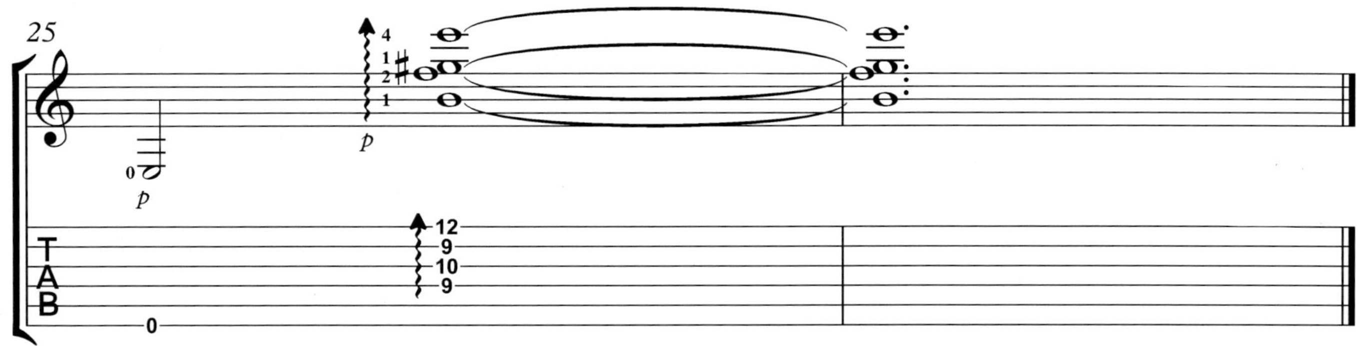
25
0
p
4
1
2
1
p
T
A
B
12
9
10
9
0

Tremolo Study II

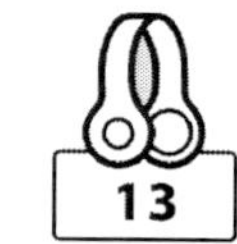

Music by YAGO SANTOS

Vivace ♩=140

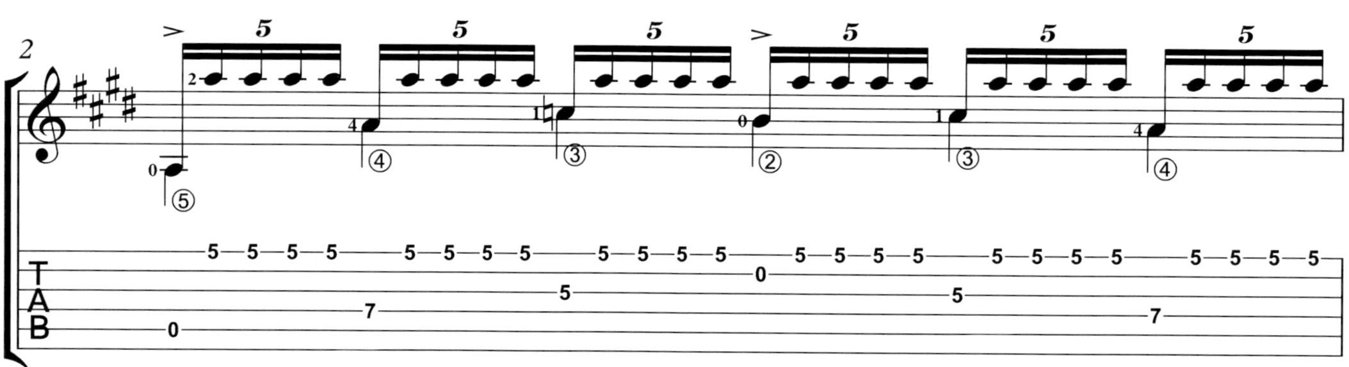

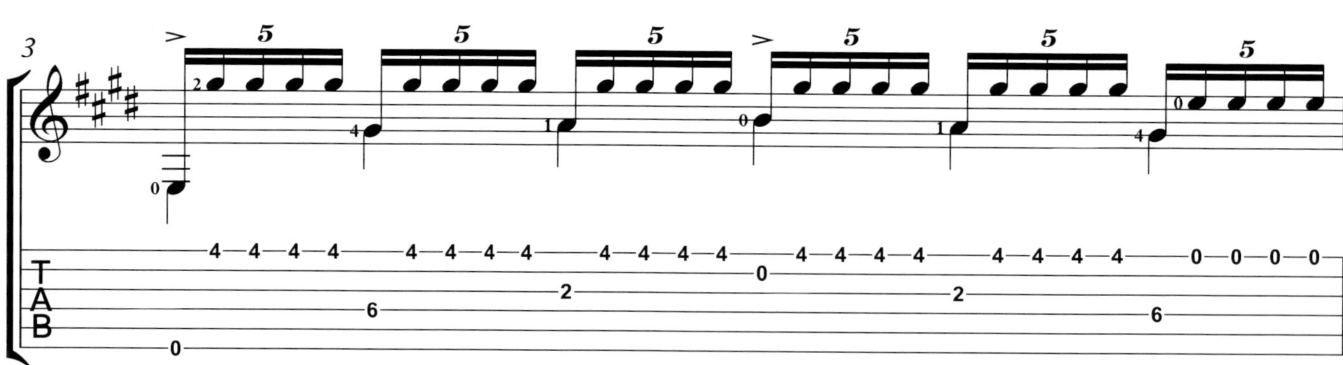

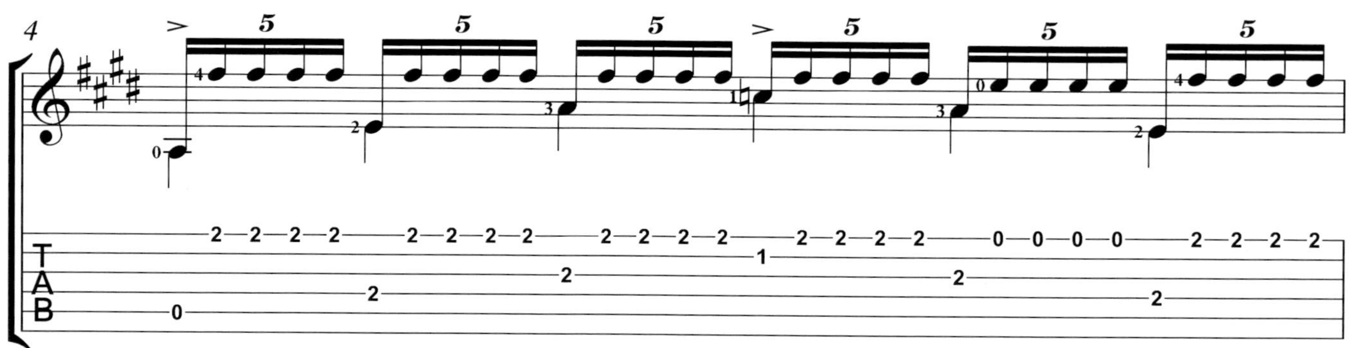

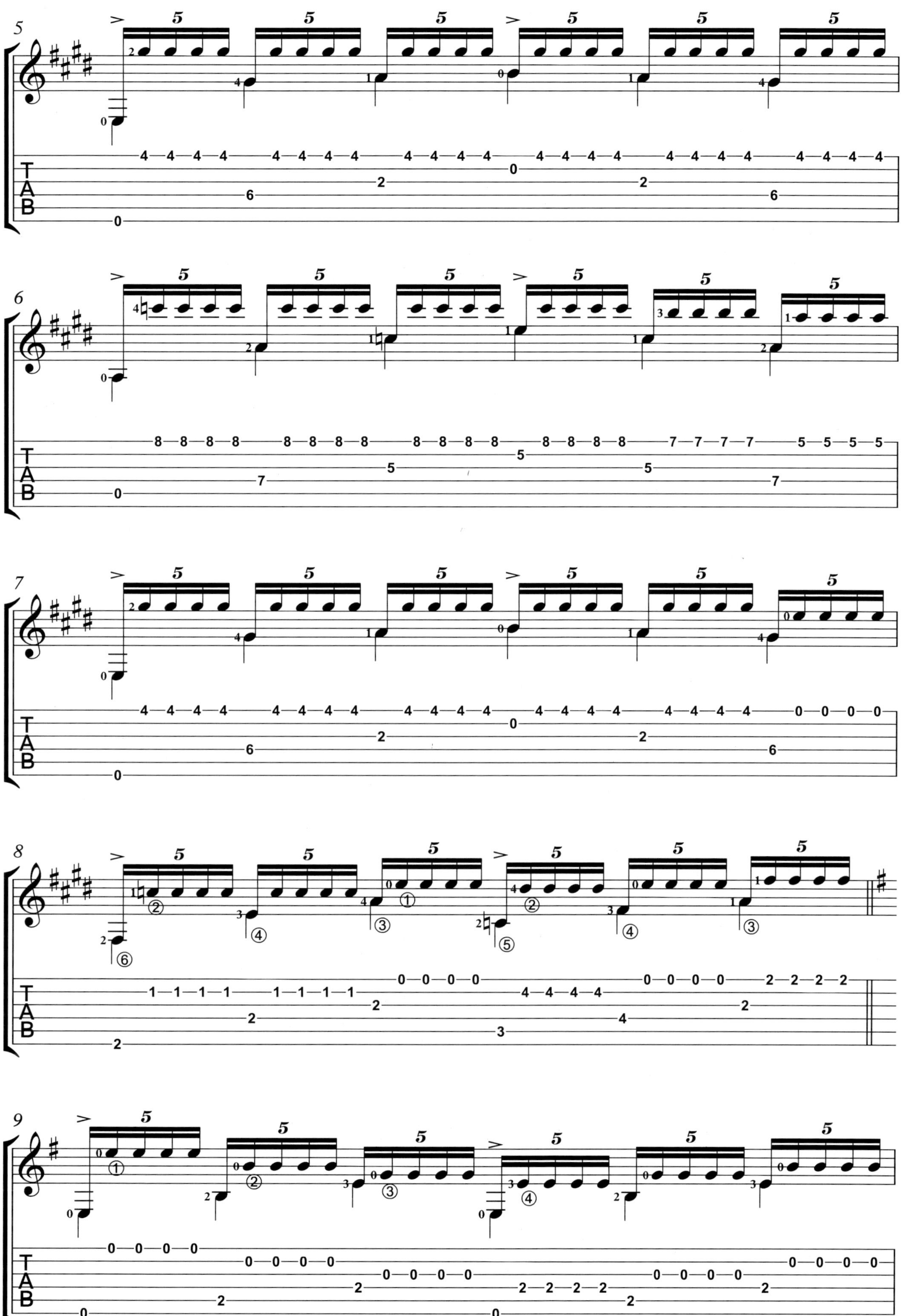

5
6
7
8
9
T
A
B

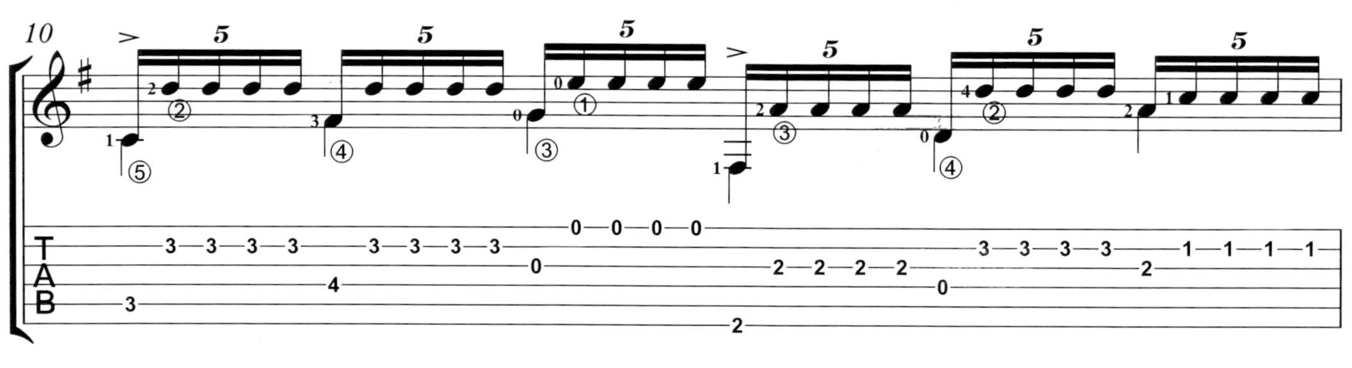
10

11

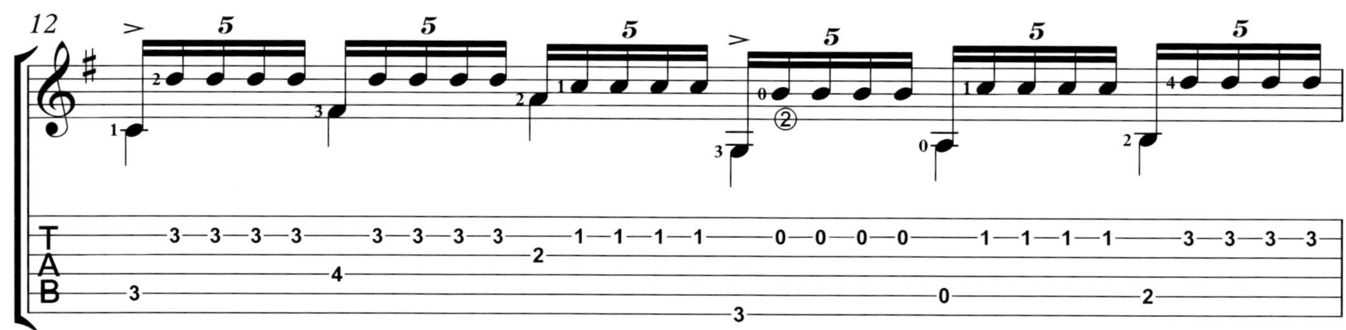
12

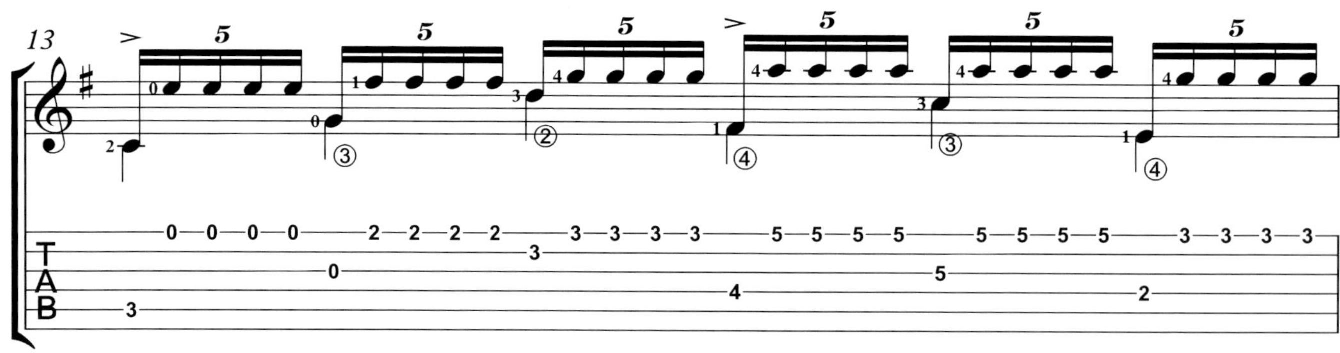
13

14

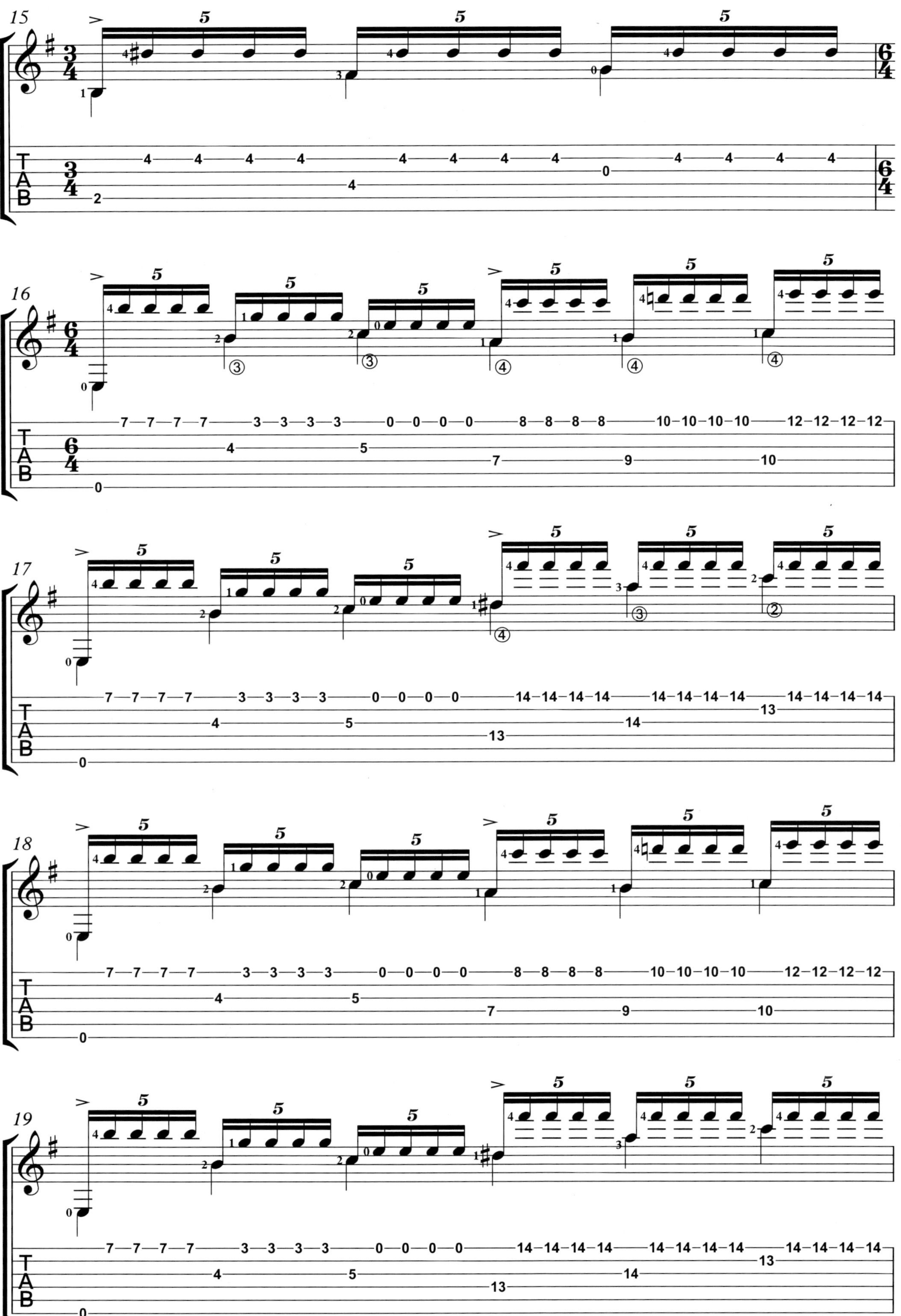

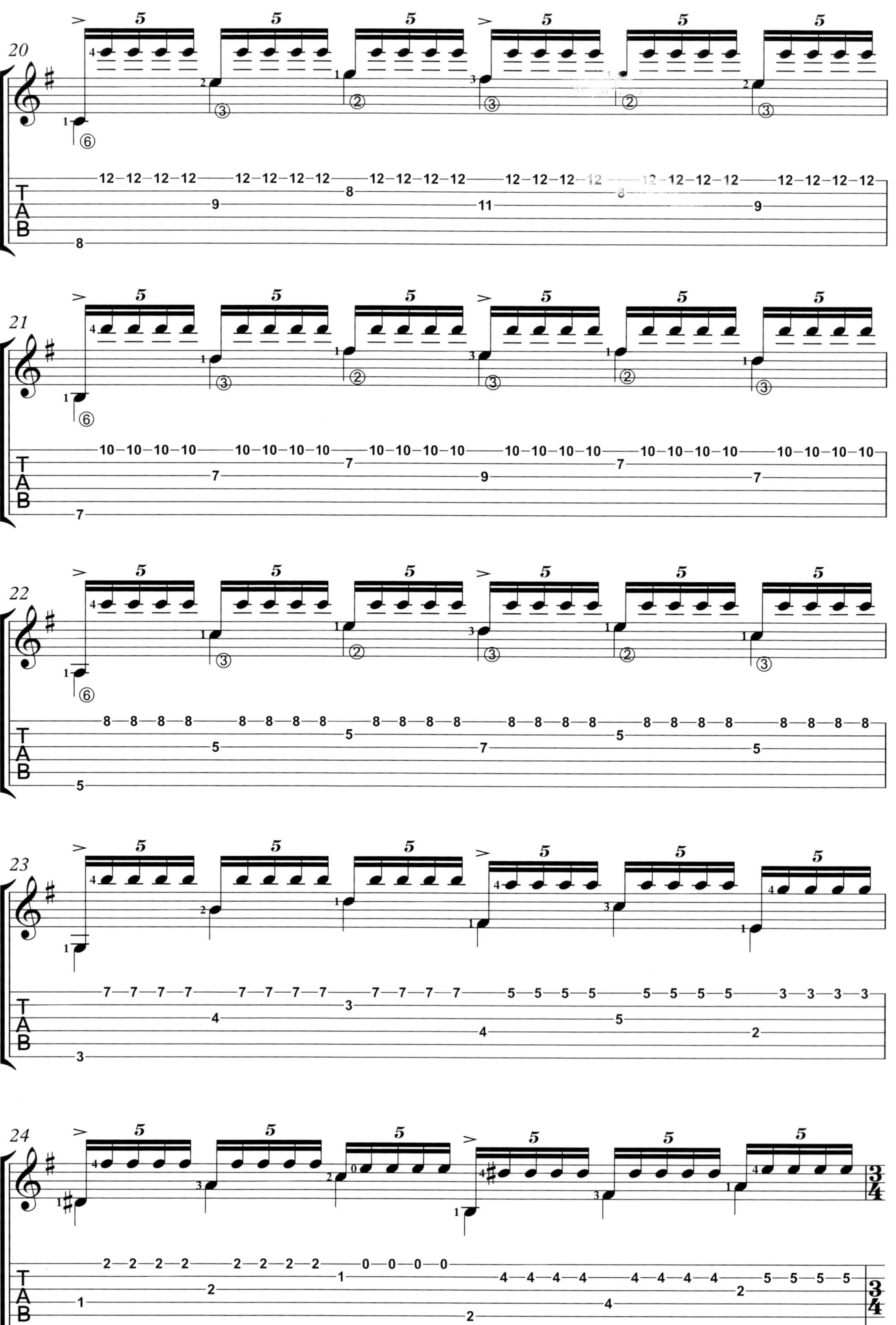

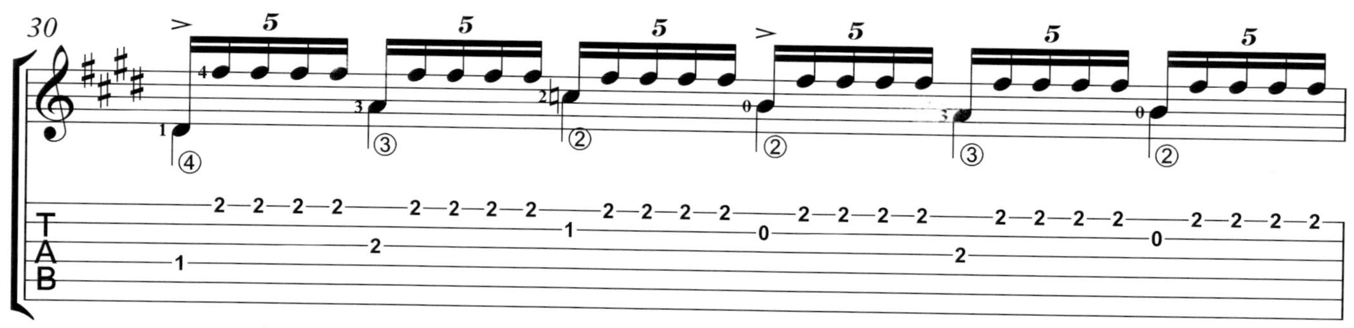
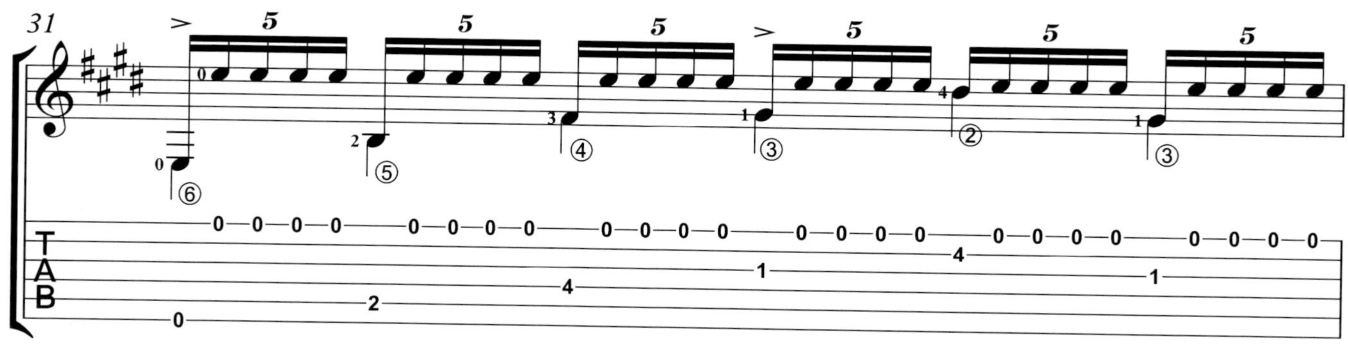
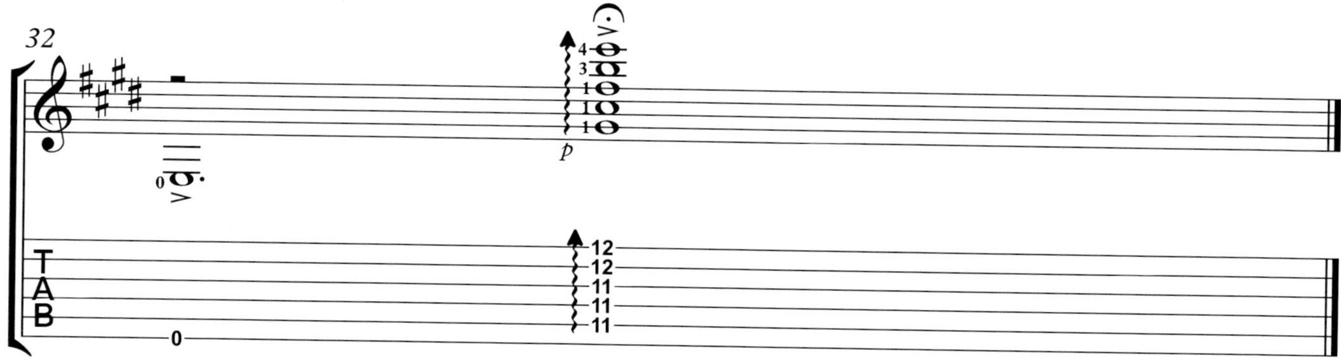

This page has been left blank to avoid an awkward page turn.

Alzapua Study I

Alzapua - Using the thumb exclusively to downstroke a single melodic note or chord, followed by rapid down-up strokes on two or more strings; with the 3rd triplet note supplied by a left-hand legato.

Music by YAGO SANTOS

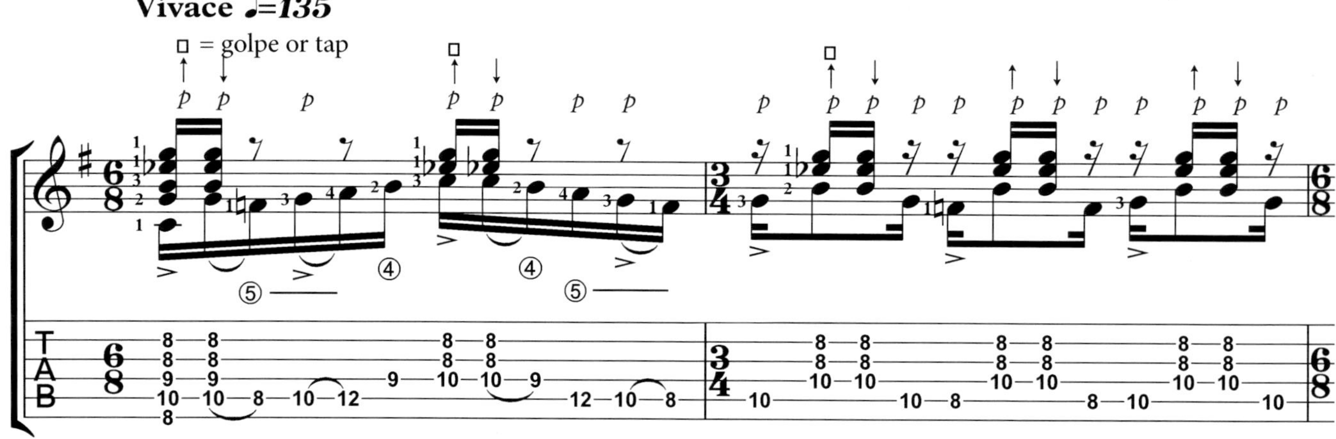

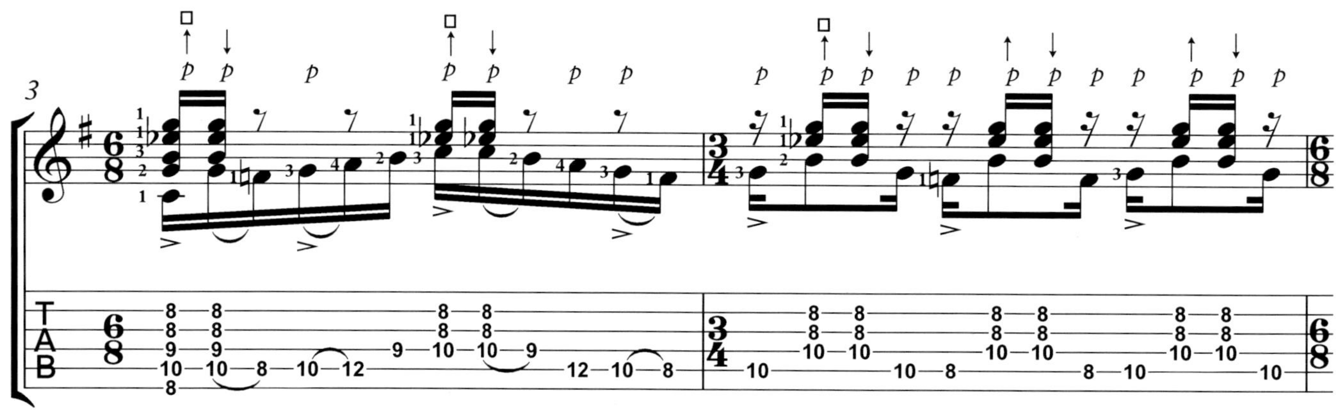

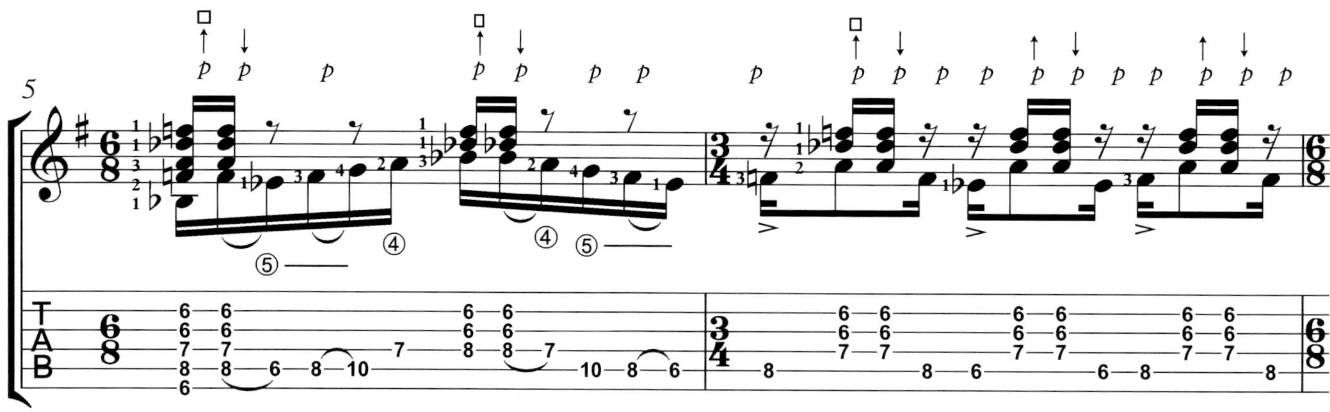

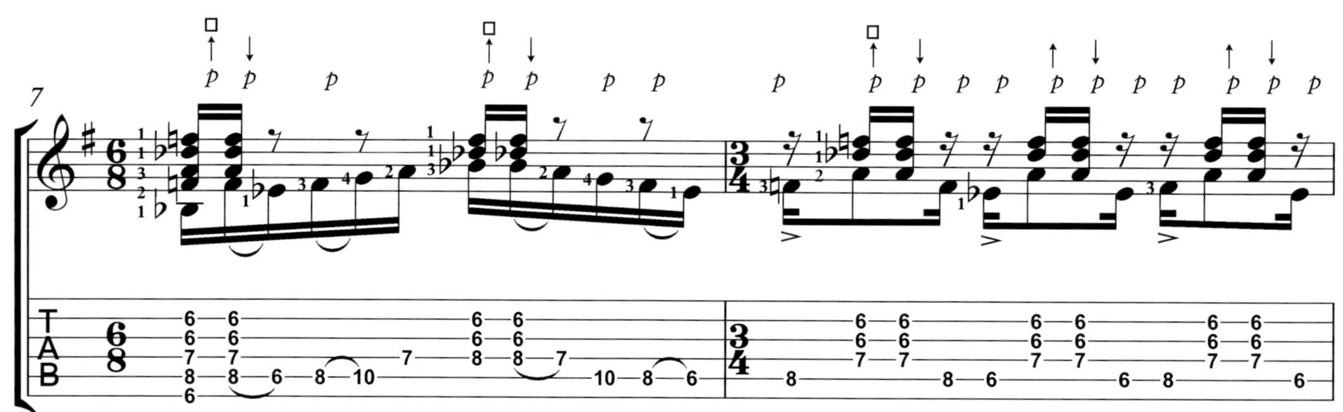

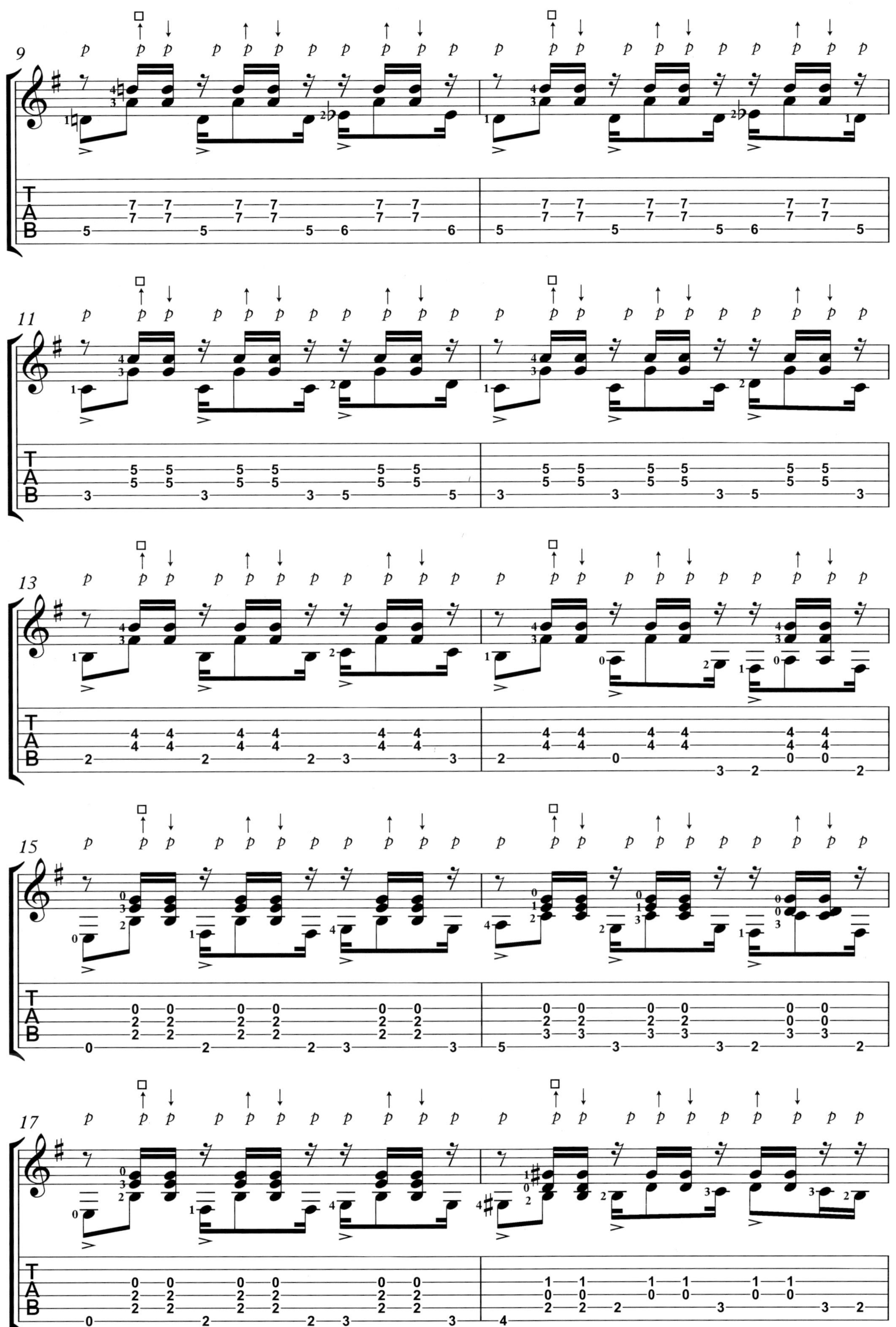

29
31
33
35
37

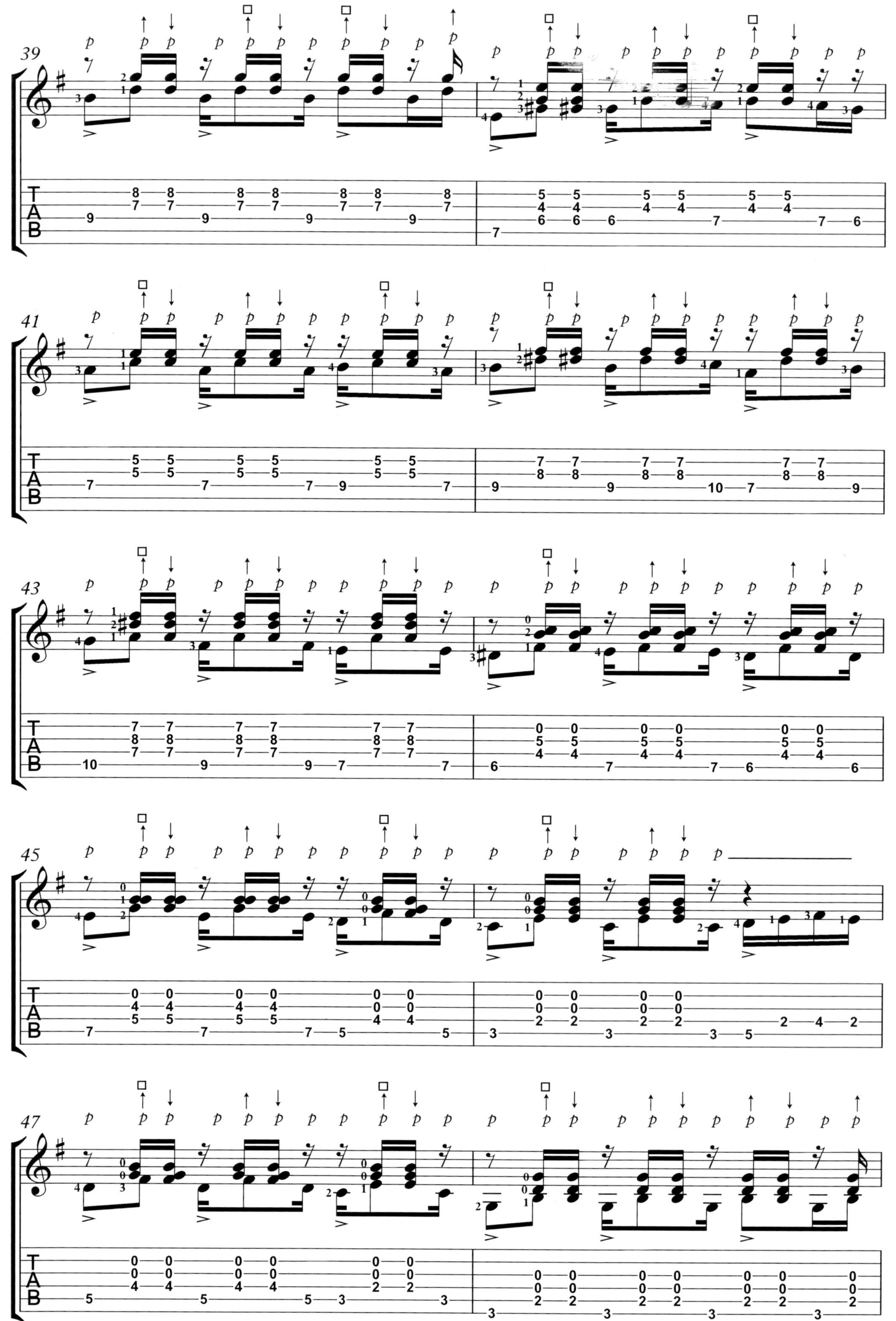

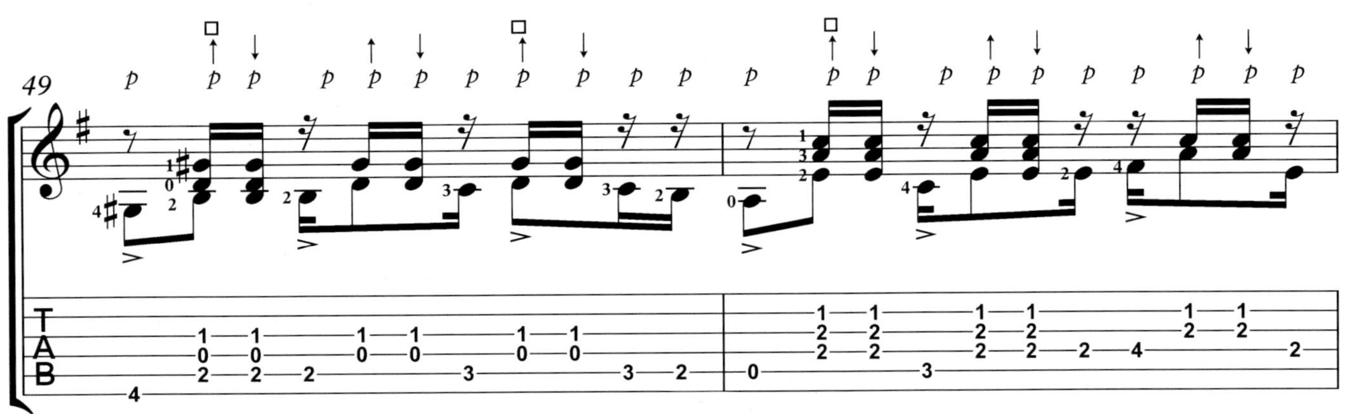
49
TAB

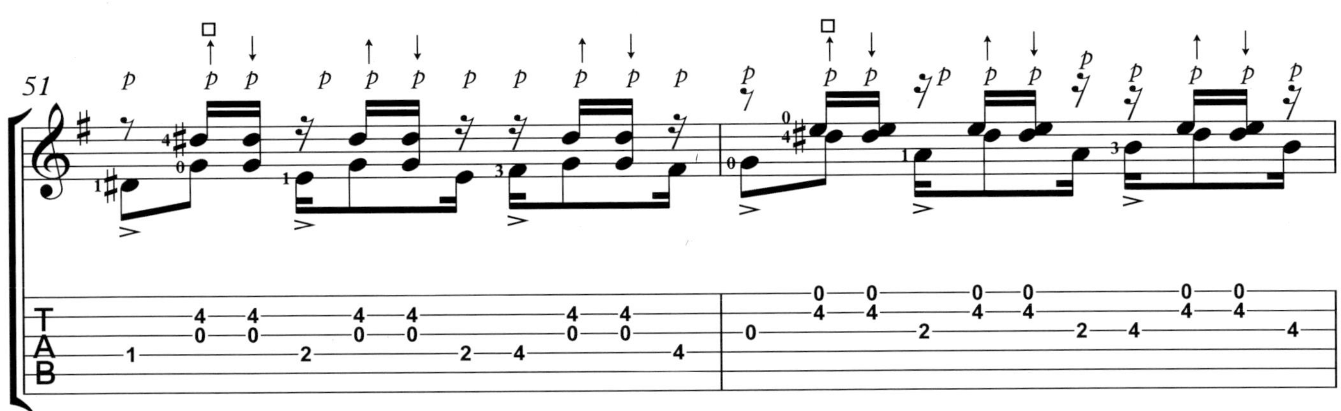
51
TAB

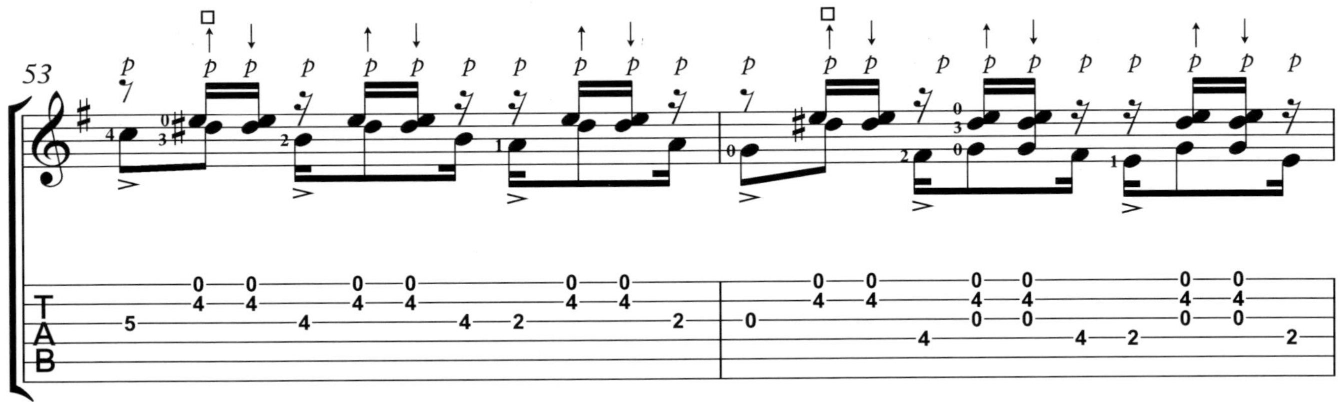
53
TAB

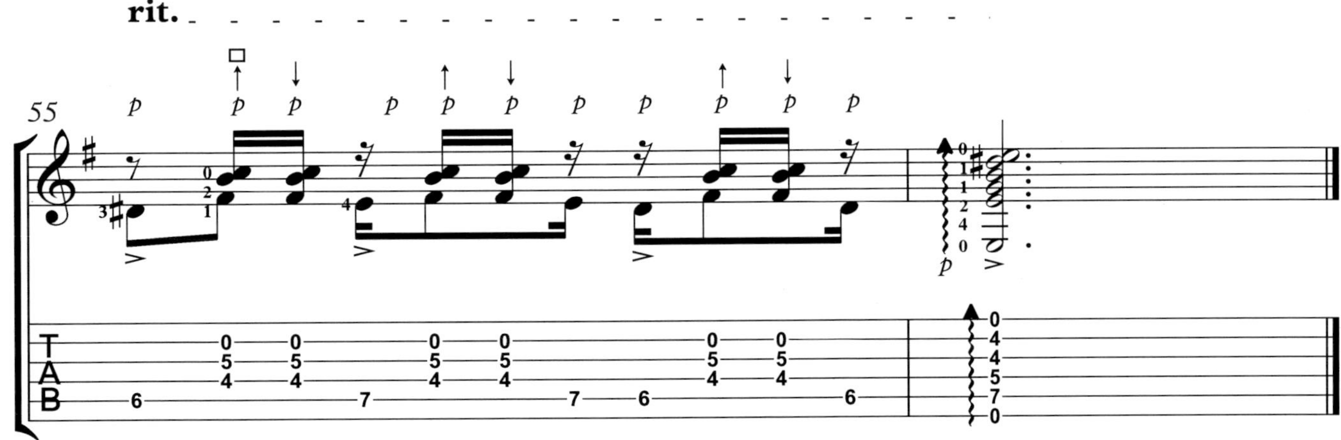
rit.
55
TAB

Alzapua-Ligado Study

Music by YAGO SANTOS

Vivace ♩=135

□ = golpe or tap

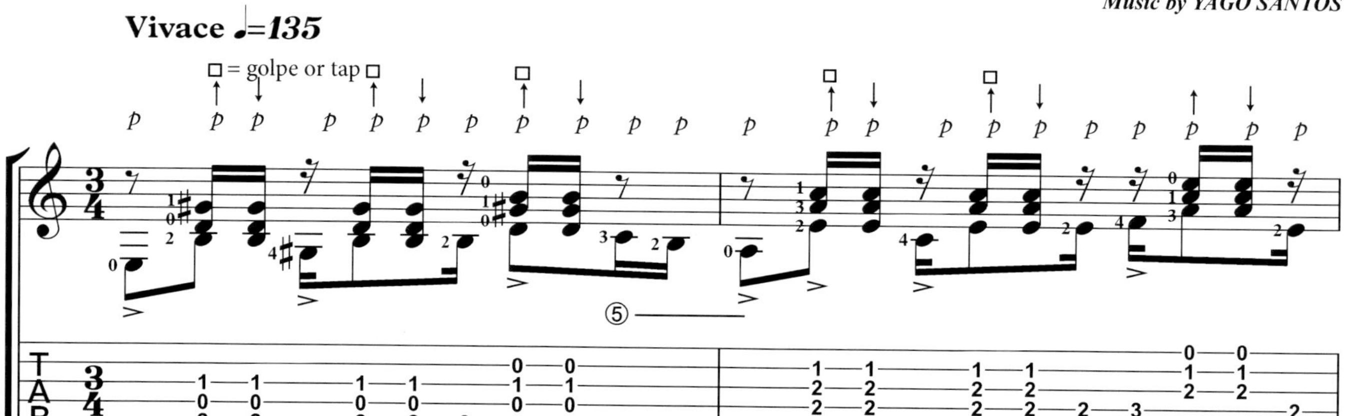

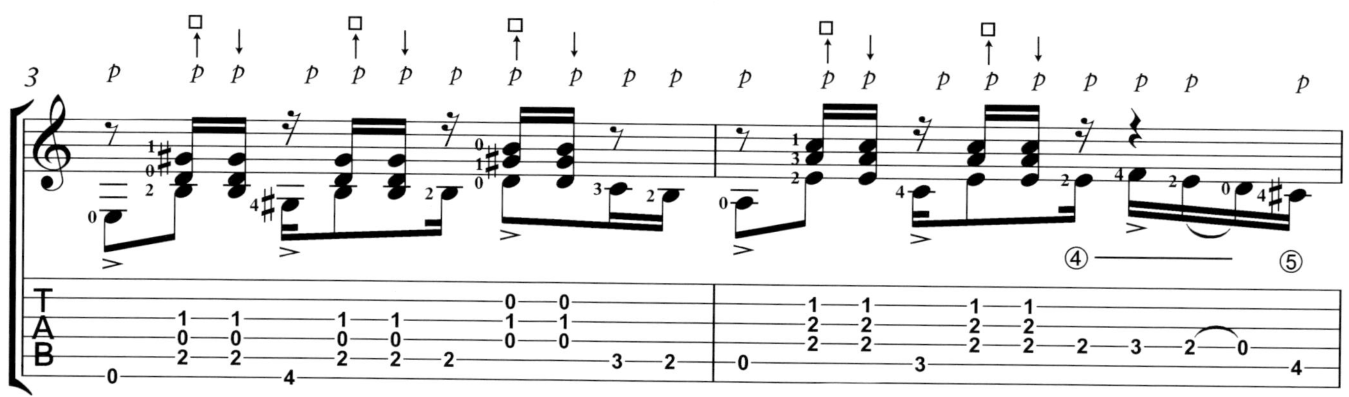

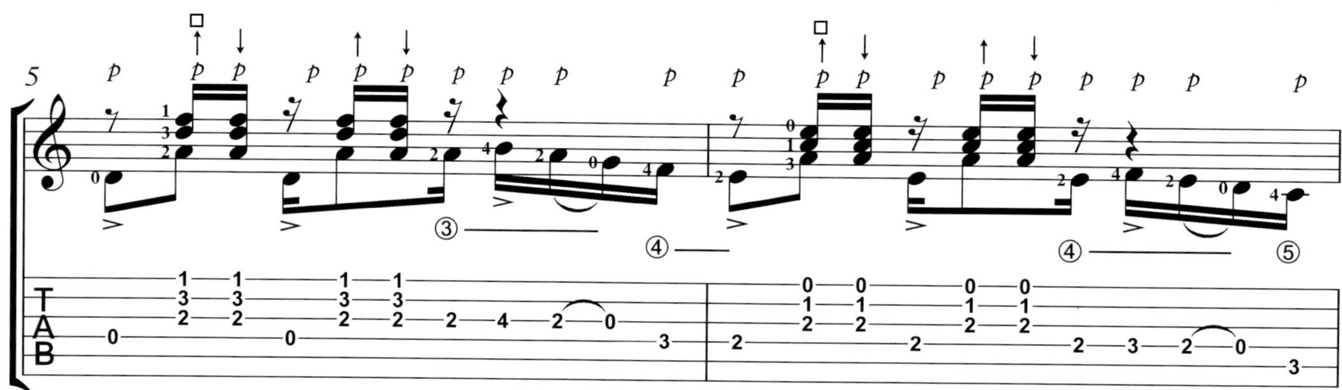

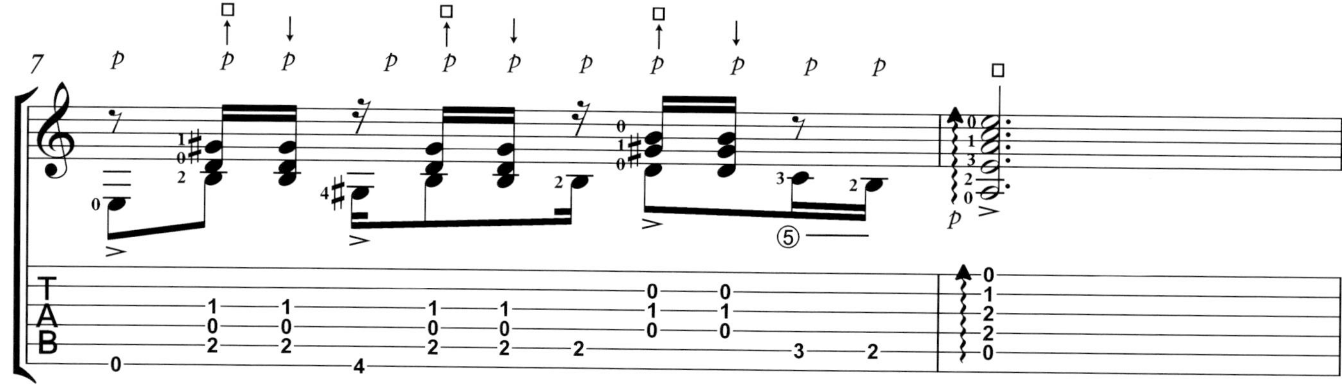

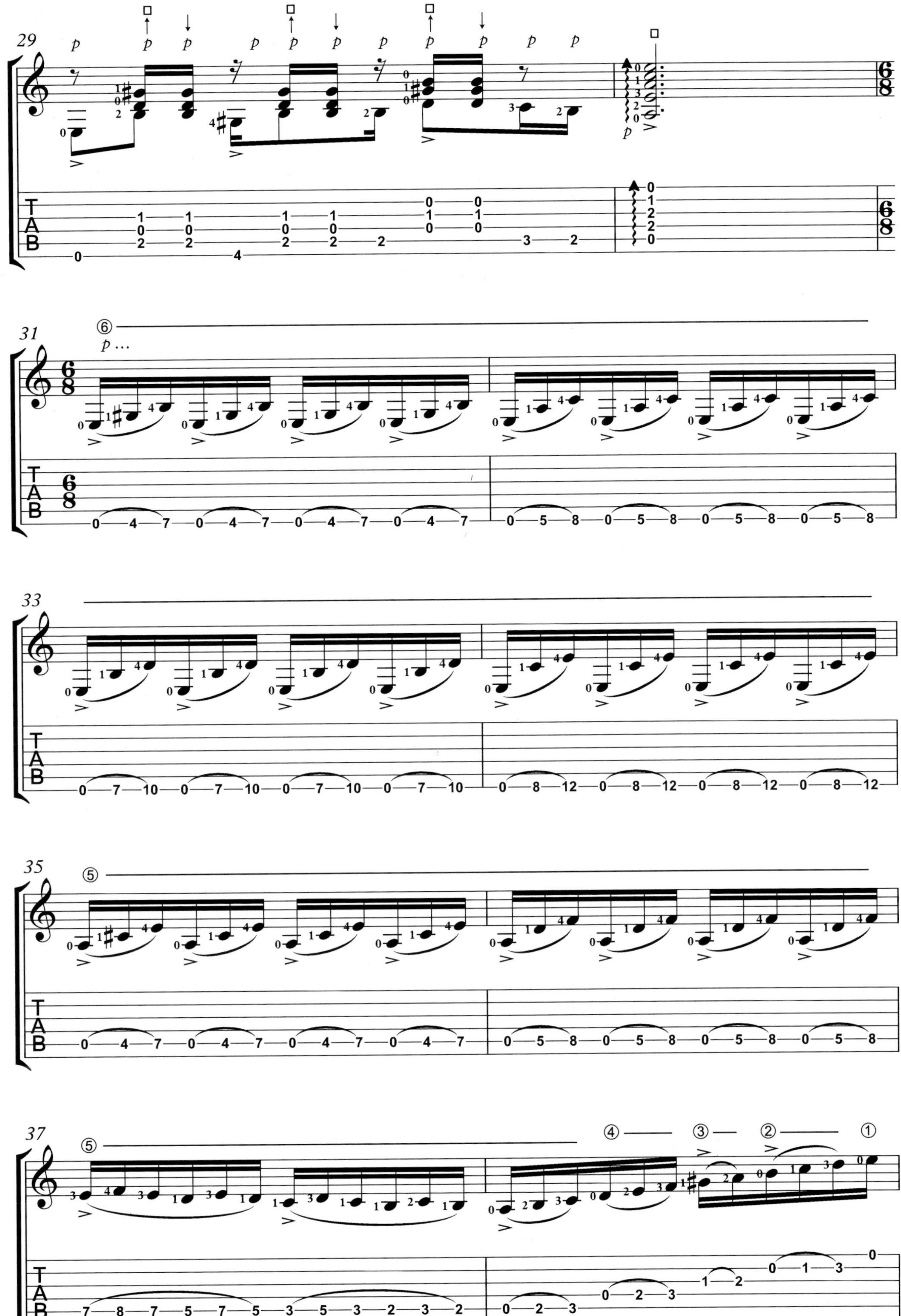

p … sigue

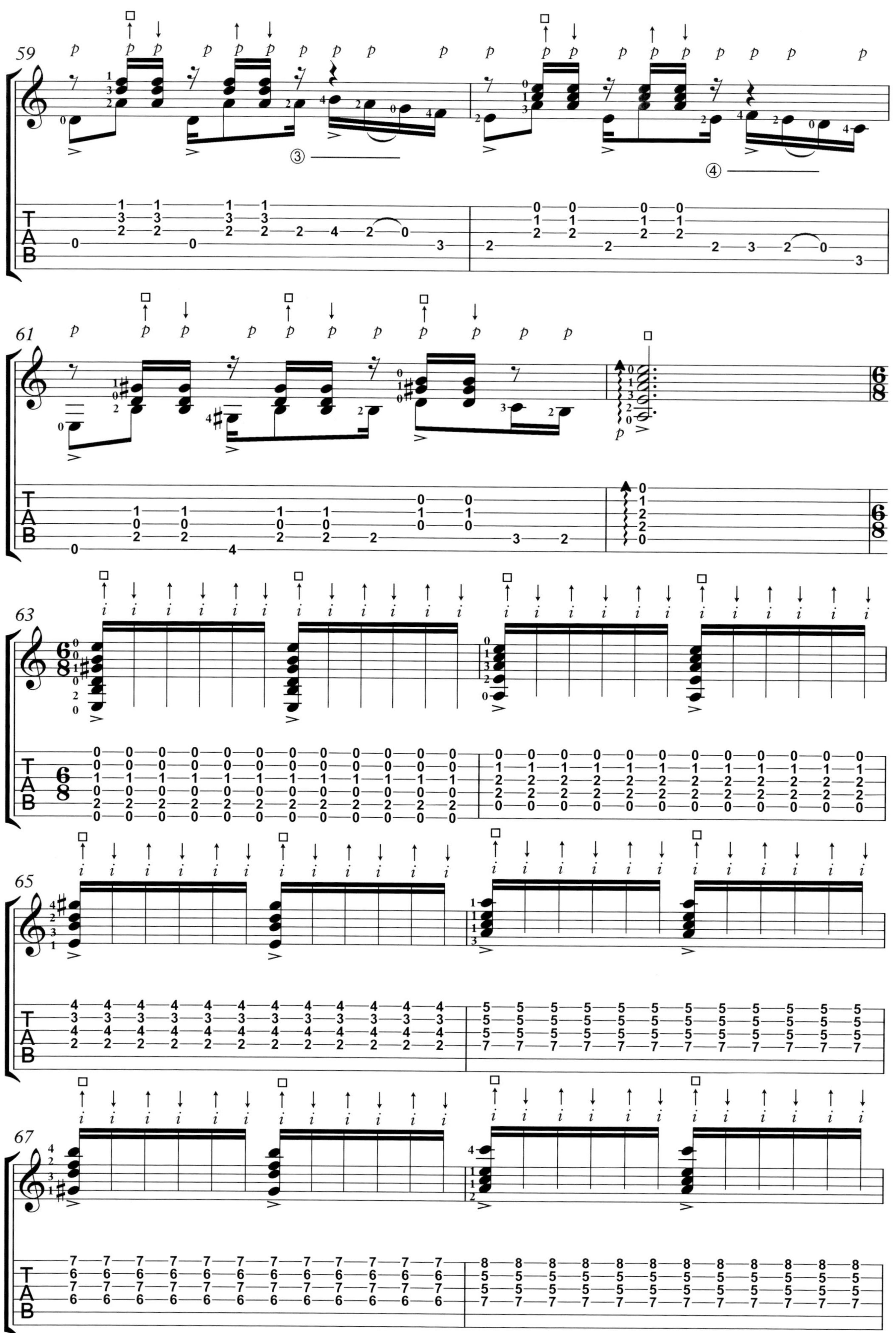

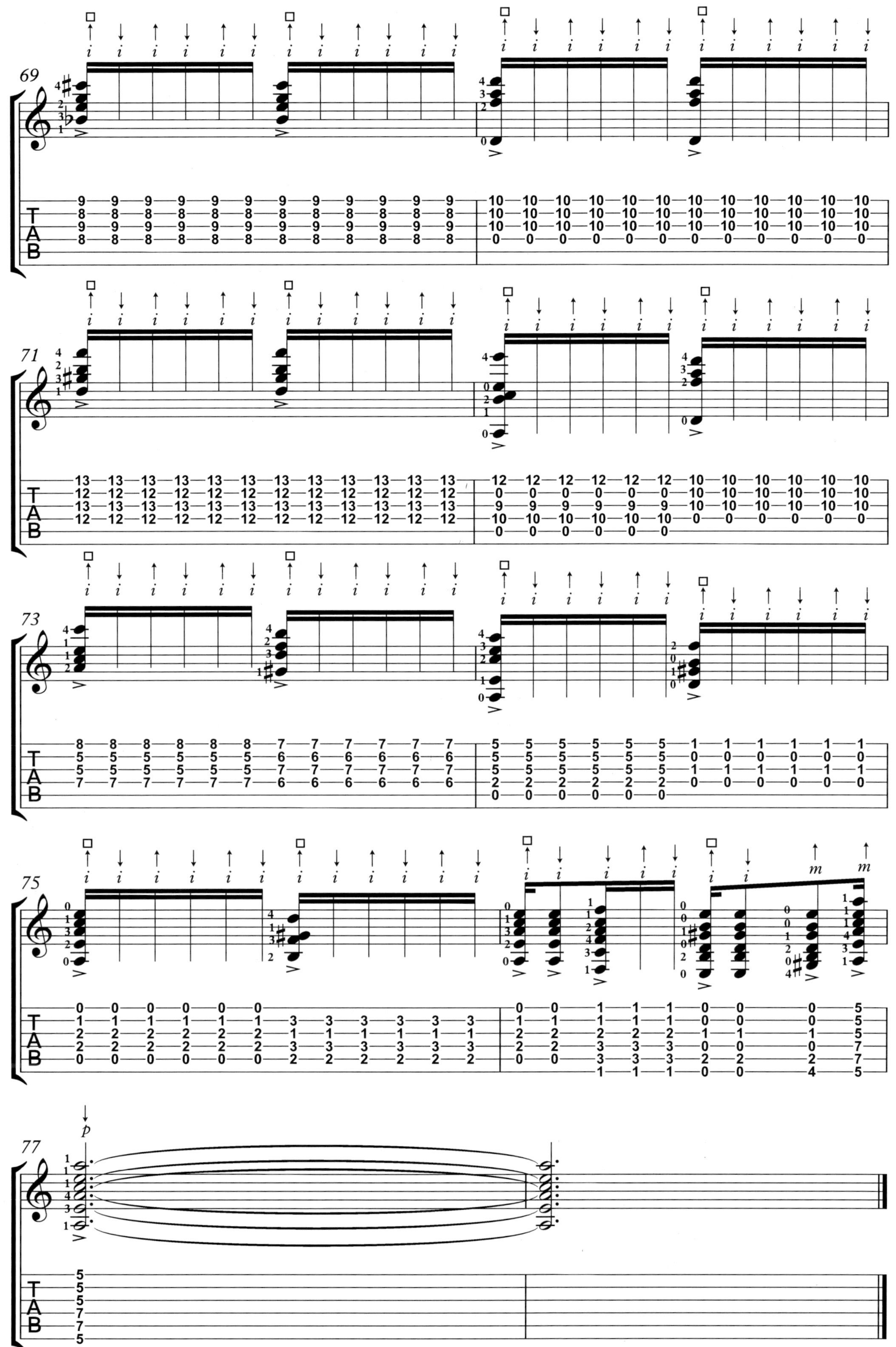
69
71
73
75
77

Ligado Study

Music by YAGO SANTOS

Allegretto ♩=100

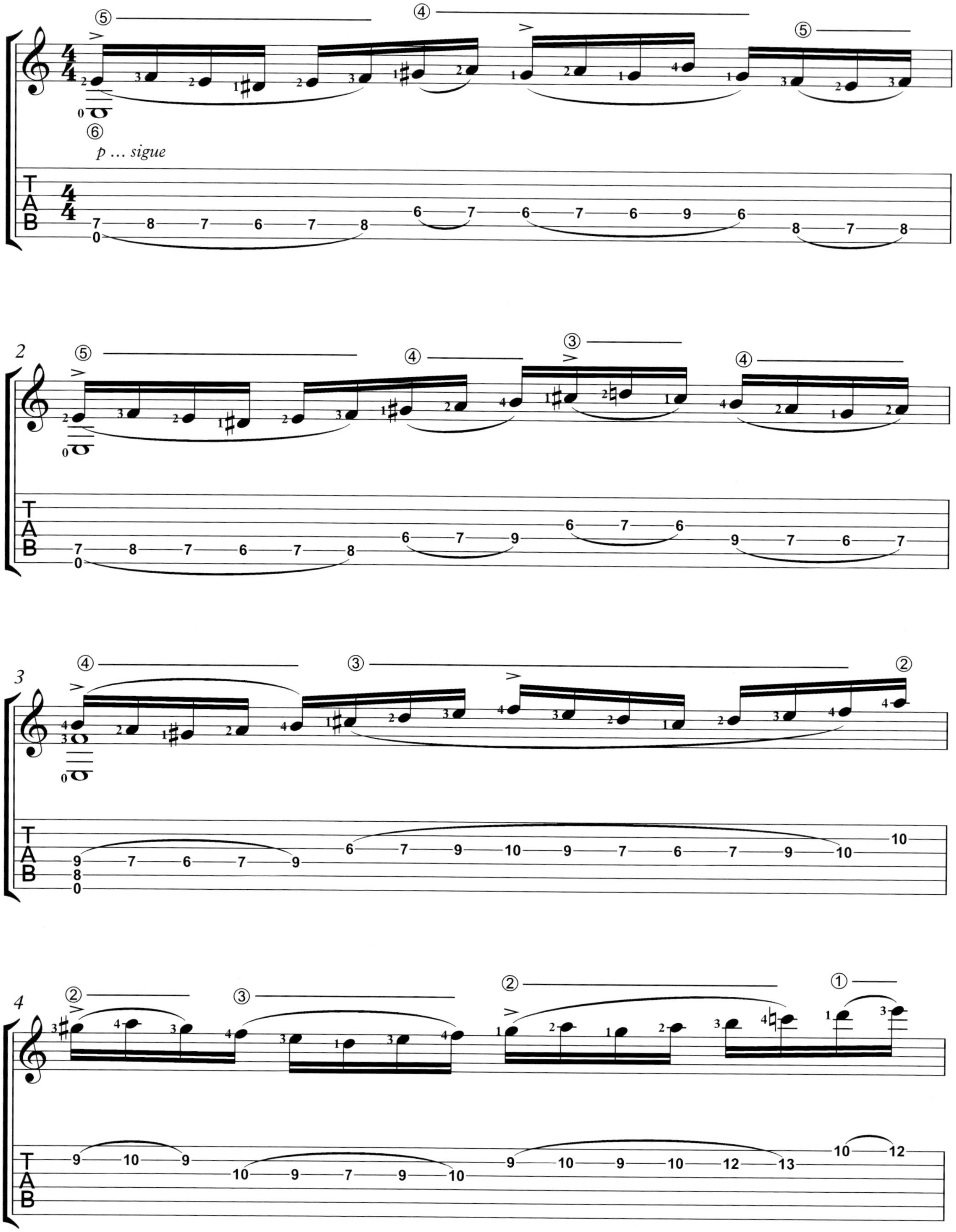

p … sigue

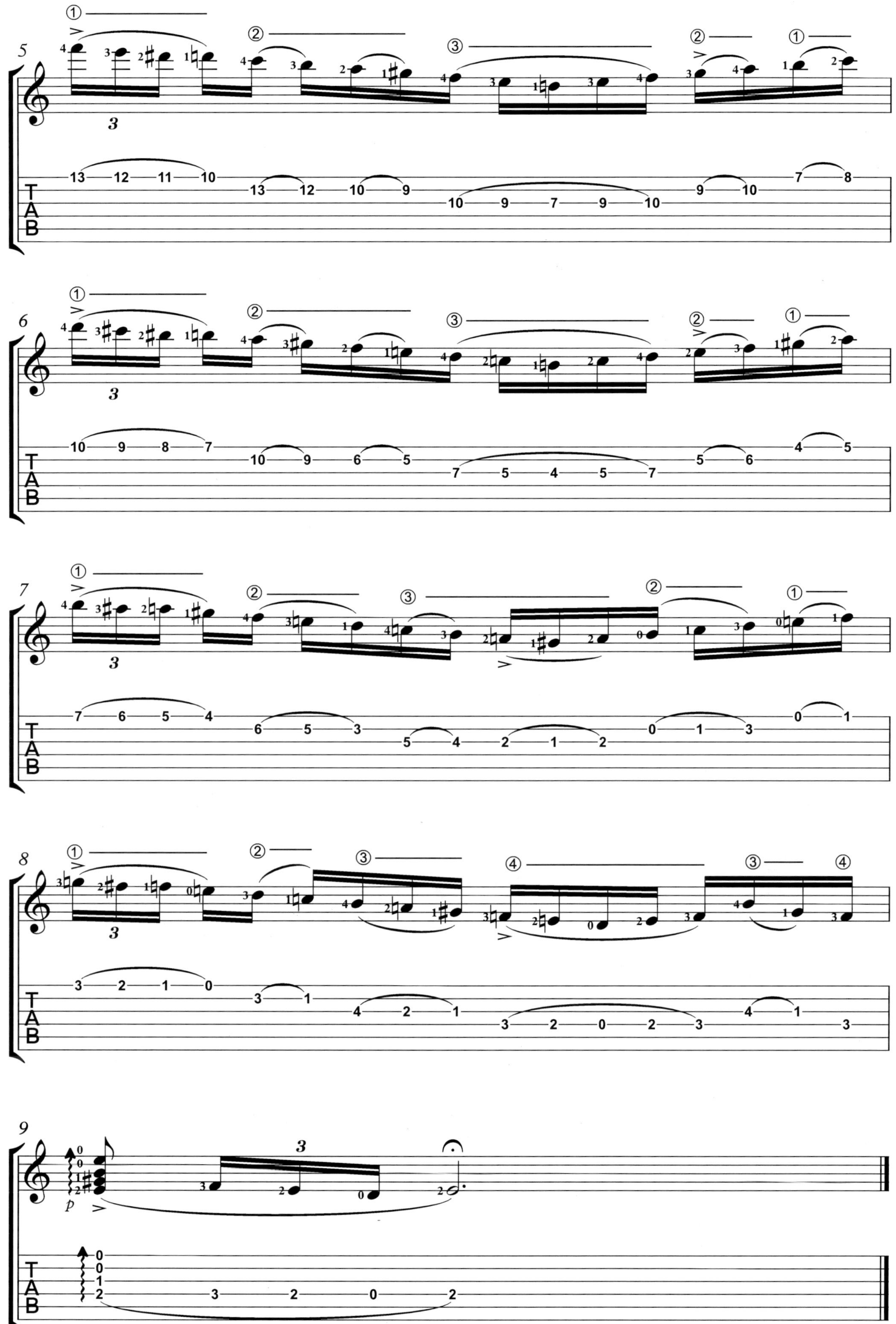

ABOUT THE AUTHOR

Yago Santos has toured internationally as a soloist and shared the stage with flamenco artists such as José Mercé, Manuel Molina, Rafael Riqueni, El Pele, José el de la Tomasa and Mayte Martín. He won the first international Paco de Lucía Prize at the Seville International Guitar Competition and collaborated with Hans Zimmer and Lorne Balfe on the EMI-nominated *National Geographic* series, *Genius: Picasso*. Yago is a disciple of maestro Rafael Riqueni and is a summa cum laude graduate of the prestigious Berklee College of Music (Boston). In 2021 he released his first album *Alma de Niño* with the record label Karonte.

Photo by Diego Gallardo